for the Girls of Kent Place — Winners all —

But Everyone Else *Looks so Sure* of Themselves

A Guide to Surviving the Teen Years

Denise V. Lang

With love!
Denise Lang
April 1991

SHOE TREE PRESS
WHITE HALL, VIRGINIA

Other Books by Denise V. Lang

Family Harmony: Coping with Your "Challenging" Relatives
*The Phantom Spouse: Helping You and Your Family Survive Business
     Travel and Relocation*
Footsteps in the Ocean: Careers in Diving

Published by Shoe Tree Press, an imprint of
Betterway Publications, Inc.
P.O. Box 219
Crozet, VA 22932
(804) 823-5661

Cover design and photograph by Susan Riley
Typography by Park Lane Associates

Library of Congress Cataloging-in-Publication Data

Lang, Denise V.
    But everyone else looks so sure of themselves : a guide to
    surviving the teen years / by Denise V. Lang.
        p. cm.
    Includes index.
    Summary: Gives advice to teens on how to deal with many of the
    troubles, conflicts, and situations frequently encountered in
    adolescence.
    ISBN 1-55870-177-X
        1. Teenagers—United States—Juvenile literature. 2. Adolescence—
    Juvenile literature. [1. Interpersonal relations. 2. Conduct of life.] I.
    Title.
    HQ796.L29 1990
    305.23′5--dc20   90-39087
                                                                    CIP
                                                                    AC

Printed in the United States of America
0 9 8 7 6 5 4 3 2 1

*For Tiffany Marie
and Christopher Clark,
who served not only as my inspiration
but as my first editors on this book.*

Acknowledgments

There are many people who cringe when you mention adolescence ... and then there are those who dedicate their lives to helping adolescents find the best in themselves. I have had the privilege of using the expert knowledge of some of those dedicated people in this book.

Special thanks go to three talented New Jersey Family Life educators: Carol Adamsbaum, at Parsippany Hills High School; Kathy Wilderson, at The Peck School; and Susan Cote, at Kent Place School. Also to Joan Howard, past president of the StepFamily Association of America and family therapist, and Rosemarie Kopacsi, adolescent therapist and family counselor who was helpful in getting my thoughts and priorities organized.

Thanks goes to Dr. Miller Newton, founder of KIDS, Inc., who has dedicated his life to making sure that kids become drug-free and functioning again, and Detective Anthony Soranno of the Morris Township Police Department, who handles kids with sensitivity and intelligence. Finally, a debt of thanks goes to Susan Wilson, executive coordinator for New Jersey Family Life Education and pioneer in the area of bringing good information about life to adolescents everywhere.

This book could not have been done without the encouragement and guidance of these special people who see adolescence as an important and exciting stage of life.

Table of Contents

Table of Contents

Introduction

Thirteen-year-old D. and her parents had had a big fight.

During the course of the argument, her father had yelled, "What do you mean you have problems? You don't know what real problems are, young lady!"

Later, much later . . . after all the screaming and door-slamming and tears had quieted, D. sat down to write her parents a letter.

> Dear Mom and Dad,
>
> I really don't know how to begin this letter. I'm sorry for the way I acted. After my head cleared I realized what a brat I acted like and how it looked to you. I can understand your side of the story but I'd like you to try and understand my side too.
>
> Sometimes, lately especially, I feel that the whole world is closing in on me. I have to do this and that just right and, I don't know — I just get sick of trying; trying in school, trying to be polite, trying to look nice, trying to do things right in general, and honestly, at times I feel that no matter how hard I try, I can't seem to do *anything* right. So I guess I try to break loose and act like a brat, which I know is no reason and I realize it afterwards, but not at the time I'm doing it.

The letter continued to explain her need for some time alone to think things through once in a while. She closed it on a hopeful note . . .

> Well, that's the story and now you know what a lunatic you must have for a daughter. I love you.
>
> D.

D.'s father was wrong in a way. Anyone who is between the ages of ten and fifteen (And there are ten million of you according to the government!) knows what real problems are. Real problems are when nobody at home respects your privacy and feelings. Or when your best friend dumps you to hang out with your worst enemy. Real problems are when you can't seem to get along with your new stepfamily or when everyone else's body and social life is developing, but yours is stuck on "start." And a real problem is when you get involved in a romantic relationship and then start to feel pressure to do things you may not feel you are ready for.

These are all real problems when you are in that crazy period called adolescence. Adolescence is a period of life that we all have to pass through — kind of like losing your baby teeth to make way for the adult teeth in your mouth. But the physical change is just one part of it. The real problems come from the emotional changes and the decisions that you are called upon to make.

And that's why I wrote this book especially for you.

When we go through adolescence, it is easy to feel that everyone else has all the answers while we are falling apart inside. Added to that are the decisions you have to face in your contemporary world — drugs, alcohol, crime, sex, pressure to do well in school, and much more.

In preparing to write this book, I not only talked to those adults who are experts in dealing with adolescents, I went to the *real* experts — the adolescents themselves. I talked to, or surveyed, hundreds of kids from New Jersey, Michigan, Wisconsin, Florida, California, and even Hawaii. Most of the kids were between the ages of ten and seventeen. They gave me very honest answers to some very tough questions. The stories that you will read are all true, but the names have all been changed to protect the person's privacy.

The result is a practical guide that will do three things:

- It will address the real problems you are facing today;
- It will arm you with three secret weapons to make you a powerful decision-maker;
- It will let you know that *you are not alone* in your problems.

By the way, when I was putting all of my material together, I came across D.'s letter. It sounded so much like what I was hearing from the adolescents I had talked to, I decided to include it . . . even though this is 1990 and I wrote that letter to my parents in 1963!

You *are not* alone, and you *can* make it! Good luck!

CHAPTER 1

THE CRAZIEST TIME of YOUR LIFE!

Eleven-year-old Carrie had been dreading having to give her book report. Her stomach hurt, her ankles were shaking, and she was sure everyone would notice the pimples forming on her chin. When it was finally her turn, she made her way up to the front of the classroom. She faced the class and opened her mouth to speak, but no words came out. She was so nervous, she threw up instead and ran from the classroom. "I can never face them again!" she cried.

Twelve-year-old Bill spent all afternoon raking the front lawn leaves and bagging them. Then he went around and picked up any bits of garbage he found — all without being asked. He could just imagine how surprised and pleased his father was going to be when he arrived home. Bill's father got home late that day, though, after a bad day at the office. He did not notice the great job Bill had done outside, but he did notice that Bill's room was a mess and yelled at him for it. Hurt and angry, Bill yelled back, "You never pay attention to the good things I do! Well, I don't care about you either!"

It took thirteen-year-old Sara nearly six weeks to get up enough courage to speak to Jason, a cute boy in her class. She was shy and didn't know what to say. Jason was popular and seemed friendly with everyone. Sara would imagine all the smart and funny things she would say that would make Jason be as crazy about her as she was about him. Finally, after days of planning, Sara took the opportunity to talk to Jason by his locker. None of her friends were around and he seemed to be alone too.
  "Jason?" she asked.
  "Yes?" he said, turning to face her.
  Sara was so nervous that, instead of speaking, she cut loose with the loudest fart she had ever heard! Everyone within twenty-five feet started laughing and pointing at her. Sara, totally embarrassed, ran down the hall. She avoided Jason for the rest of the year.

Isn't it awful to have frustrating and embarrassing moments like those? Your life may seem to be filled with them. Not only embarrassing moments, but feelings of anger, joy, resentment, hurt, confusion, self-consciousness, a desire to be recognized, independence, and just wanting to hide from the world. If this sounds contradictory — it is. Welcome to the world of adolescence — the craziest time of your life. But it can be the most exciting time, as well.

Do you remember when your kindergarten or nursery school teacher brought a butterfly larva to school and the entire class watched each day as the caterpillar spun a cocoon around itself? You could only imagine the wonderful changes that must be going on inside that golden pod. It was hard waiting those weeks for the butterfly to emerge. Then one day, it happened! You went to school and instead of that plain shell there was a gorgeous butterfly with iridescent wings and brilliant shades of gold, purple, blue, red, orange, and green! What a change!

Well, that is what is happening to you now. The child that you were is changing and this change is explosive. Your body is growing and changing, your emotions are taking off in new directions, and you are finding that you have to make decisions about right and wrong that are not always easy.

Unlike the butterfly, however, which does its changing in the privacy of its cocoon, you—the adolescent—are changing right out in public! Right out where others can see you when you goof up. Right out where others tell you what to do when you really want to make your own decisions. Right out where others expect you to perform when you aren't even sure of your abilities yet.

And what everyone else expects of you seems to change from day to day and even hour to hour!

How Others View You

"I was sitting at the end of the lunch table and I took a zip-lock bag full of sliced apples and tried to see if it really worked," said fourteen-year-old Heather. "When I shook the bag around like they do on TV, the apples flew across the whole lunch room. They knocked down milks and hit people in the head — including a teacher! I was so embarrassed. I can imagine what they thought of me!"

What words come to mind when your age group is described by adults? "Oh, he's at *that* stage. You know — obnoxious, loud, selfish, argumentative, and rotten!" "She's at that rebellious age!" "He used to be such a nice kid, but one day he woke up and a monster had taken his place!"

Try this on the adults you know. Ask any of them if they could pick any age to be, what age would they pick? Then ask them if they would like to be twelve or thirteen or fourteen again. Guess what they'll say? Most likely it will be either: "No way!" or "Sure, I'd be thirteen again, but only if I could be thirteen knowing what I know now!"

What adults "know now" that they didn't know at your age is, first, that they will live through it — all the changes, anxieties, embarrassments, and emotions — and second, how to cope with all those situations in which you find yourself for the first time! That's it! That's the big secret — learning how to cope. But that's what you are going to learn as you read this book!

How You View Yourself

Mark's father is a successful businessman. He is also a skillful tennis player and vice-president of his town's chamber of commerce. He jogs regularly to stay fit and does crossword puzzles in ink, rarely leaving a blank box. It seems that he can talk to anyone about anything . . . except to Mark. Thirteen-year-old Mark feels he will never measure up to what his father is or what his father expects Mark to be. This makes Mark angry, so lately he's refused to play tennis with his dad. After all, he can't beat him and he is tired of his father continually pointing out what he is doing wrong. In fact, Mark doesn't have much to do with his father if he can help it. This, of course, makes Mark's dad angry and the two have been fighting a lot.

As you start to stretch physically, mentally, and emotionally towards adulthood, it is natural to compare yourself to the adults closest to you. For someone like Mark, it may be a parent. For others, it is another relative, a teacher, or a coach. In most cases, you may find yourself getting frustrated that you don't measure up to either your own expectations or theirs. It is natural to compare, but it is not realistic to expect to measure up.

Have you ever seen a house under construction? It's a real mess! A few of the walls may be up but the frame is exposed in other places and insulation hangs out so that it gets wet in the rain. It's hard to tell what the rooms and floors are going to look like through all the dirt, cement, and dust. There are no finishing touches such as paint, wallpaper, or appliances and the outside looks even worse. There is lots of mud and truck tire marks and no trees or plants to make it beautiful. In fact, you wonder how this will *ever* look like the house next door, with its cheery kitchen, neat yard, and welcoming color. But eventually, it will. In fact, it may even be bigger, warmer, and more beautiful. It's just that it is difficult to see the finished product through all the construction.

You are like that house under construction. All the parts are slowly being put into place. At this stage you can't compare yourself with the finished house next door (the adult in your life) because you aren't going to measure up. You aren't finished yet! But remember, when you *are* finished, you may find that you are brighter, more talented, and more popular than the person you now compare yourself to.

So the question is, how do you get through this period of construction and successfully deal with all the conflicts, pressures, and changes coming at you from all directions? There are three weapons for you to use.

Do a Reality Check

Students who take journalism courses either in high school or college will, at some point, be involved in a debate about whether there is such a thing as being totally objective — that is, whether one can look at a situation and simply report the facts without adding any personal views or opinions. At first glance, you might say "Well, of course, the facts are the facts. That's easy," but think about it for a minute.

Say you were a witness to a car hitting an old man downtown. The fact that a car hit an old man may be true, but depending upon where you stood to observe the accident, you might report to others that: 1. an old man walked out in front of a moving car; 2. a speeding car hit an old man because it couldn't stop; 3. the car hit the man on purpose; 4. the driver wasn't paying attention.

Your report of the facts would be influenced by your position and your observations. This is why police officers talk to as many witnesses as possible to get a true picture of the facts.

This process is called Doing a Reality Check — looking at the same incident from a number of other people's viewpoints. Doing a Reality Check will also help you cope with your stresses and conflicts. For example, let's take another look at Bill's situation at the beginning of this chapter.

Bill worked hard to surprise his dad. When his dad came home, however, Bill's hard work wasn't noticed. Instead, his dad, who had had a bad day at work, saw Bill's messy room and yelled at him for it. Bill yelled back that his dad never paid attention to the good things Bill did. And the fight was on! Time to apply the first secret weapon—Do a Reality Check.

First, Bill needed to step outside of himself for just a minute and look at the situation like a reporter would. What are the facts?

1. Bill cleaned up the yard without being asked.
2. His father came home after dark and didn't see the work that had been done.
3. Bill's father *did* see Bill's messy room.
4. Since Bill's father was grouchy from a bad day at work, he yelled at Bill.
5. Bill felt hurt and angry so he yelled back.

Did this one incident mean that Bill's dad *never* appreciated the good things Bill did? No. Did this incident mean that Bill didn't care about his dad at all? No. Did Bill yell back because his feelings were hurt? Yes. And that's an important part of the Reality Check —identifying your feelings or needs in the situation.

As we are hit with different stresses, it is very natural to be caught up in our own feelings, activities, and emotions. We sometimes think that others — particularly family members — should *know* what we are feeling, but nobody is a mind-reader. If we Do a Reality Check and look at a stressful situation as a good reporter would, we will discover that other people may see it differently — and that they don't know what it is that we are feeling or needing at that moment.

This leads to the second secret weapon, Cool Communication.

Cool Communication

When people are hurt or angry, they tend to make sweeping statements. Some of these are "hot" or explosive words which tend to make people madder rather than calmer. Some of these words are "never," "always," and "must."

When Bill told his father "You *never* pay attention to the good things I do," it made his father madder because it simply wasn't true. Bill was ignoring the fact that his dad usually *did* notice Bill's good works. It was unfair to accuse his dad of *never* paying attention to him just because of this one incident.

People of all ages make these kinds of accusations and they are not fair. The person who is accused will then hear only the unfair accusation and get angrier, rather than pay attention to the situation at hand.

The alternative is Cool Communication — using words and phrases that will calm a person down, rather than stir him up. First, if Bill had quickly Done a Reality Check, he would have realized that he was hurt that his dad didn't notice the good job he had done outside. Instead of telling his father "You never notice . . ." he could have said "Boy, my feelings are really hurt that you didn't notice what a great job I did outside, and without being asked!" Chances are very good that his dad would have stopped in his tracks right there!

Other Cool Communication phrases include "Can you listen to what I have to say?" or "I need to talk to you. Is this a good time? If not, when?" We will discuss these further in other chapters.

Finally, if you have Done a Reality Check and used Cool Communication, there is still one more secret weapon for coping with conflicts.

Take a Positive Risk

Have you ever heard the saying "There's more than one way to skin a cat?" UGH! What a gruesome image, but the idea can be applied to just about anything else. There is usually more than one way to handle something. Often, it involves a little bit of compromise. In business it is called negotiating, but negotiating is also defined as "getting through, around, or over successfully." And in order to do *that*, you have to look at — or come up with — as many options as possible.

When you begin to come up with ways (or options) to solve a problem, you have already begun to take some control of the situation. The next step is to then take an action that you feel is best, based on your feelings, facts, and options. I call this Taking a Positive Risk.

The word "risk" is often used to refer to something that is dangerous. It also refers to taking a chance and taking action. When you Take a Positive Risk, you are taking an action that will benefit you or be healthy for you. Sometimes when you Take a Positive Risk, it works out perfectly. Sometimes it doesn't. Since you are taking a chance and doing something positive for yourself though, even when it doesn't work out, you still learn something and grow from it.

Sure, you may be doing something new and it may not be the easy thing to do, but *you* will be making the choice . . . and making choices and taking action gives you power.

Bill could have applied this to his situation by telling his dad, "I know my room is a mess. I decided to do the outside of the house for you instead. How about if I have my room clean by six o'clock tomorrow?" In this way, Bill has taken control of the situation by pointing out the good he did and offering another option to his dad.

As you read through the rest of the book, you'll see how you can use these three secret weapons — Do a Reality Check, Cool Communication, and Take a Positive Risk — to help you through situations that come up at home, with friends, at school, and in your relationships with the opposite sex.

PART ONE

YOU AND YOUR FAMILY

CHAPTER 2

WHERE DO YOU FIT IN?

The place: a middle school classroom where the students had been told that a visiting author was researching a book for adolescents. **The players**: sixth and seventh graders.

"Why is it that when there is a chore to be done, my mom says 'Josh, you are *thirteen* years old. Act your age and help out!' but when I ask to do something, she says, 'You're *only* thirteen!'?"

"Yeah," agreed Monica. "And I hate it when my parents talk about me in front of other people like I am a baby — or not even there! It happened again at Thanksgiving. The whole family was at the table and we even had some company, and my parents started telling stories about me and my friends that they thought were funny. Everybody laughed but I was really embarrassed!"

"I know what you mean," sympathized Jackie. "I think parents forget that we have feelings, too! My mother yells at me in front of my friends, and at the dinner table, she turned to my uncle and said 'Can't you see she's getting fat? Don't give her any more potatoes!'"

You may be nodding your head in agreement over these statements. The common thread running through them is that the adults involved were treating the young people ... well, like babies. It was resented and rightly so. Did the adults do it because they were mean, rotten, uncaring people? Do a Reality Check! You may come to the conclusion that the parents involved were treating the young people like small children because they hadn't realized that the child was growing up!

When I met with groups of kids, or handed out surveys, I asked about their place in the family. Most started by saying they were the oldest, middle, youngest, or only child. Then they might go a little further and say, "I'm the athletic one in the family" or "I'm the clown of the family" or even "I guess I'm the troublemaker because everyone always seems to be yelling at me."

These labels that are pinned on us in our families are built up over years. They usually start when we are very young and they're difficult to change. It's not that our parents or relatives are mean, it's just that that's the way they are used to viewing us. You may not have minded being called Butterball when you were four years old, but by the time you are eleven, twelve, or thirteen, you may begin to resent that name because it doesn't fit the image you want for yourself.

Just how would you like to be thought of in your family? How would you like to be treated? Are there things about you that you feel are important and everyone seems to ignore?

Changing Your Image

Finish this sentence in your mind: I wish my parents would realize that I am really _____.

More than half the adolescents I surveyed finished it by saying "... that I am really more capable than they think." Coming in second as an answer was "... that I'm more intelligent than they think and can make decisions." And another large group answered "... that I'm trying my best." A smaller number answered "... that I am really not as intelligent/talented as they think" or "... that I am really not out to get them."

How does your answer compare with these?

"What do you mean, where do I fit in?" asked twelve-year-old Kurt. "I don't ... except maybe as a slave. *They* make all the rules. I have no say-so!"

Solution: Do a Reality Check. The reality is: it is *their* house, they are in charge. But you want more freedom. Take a Positive Risk and generate options for yourself depending on the situation and then Coolly Communicate those feelings and options.

Problem: *"I hate it when my mother makes arrangements for me to go over to Barbara's house," said Melissa. "I don't even like Barbara. Can't she see that I'm old enough to make my own decisions about who I want to spend time with?"*

Solution: Do a Reality Check. From the time you were a toddler, your mom made the arrangements for you to play with others she thought you might enjoy. The reality now is that you have definite preferences and want to make your own decisions about your social life. Coolly Communicate how you feel to your mom. For example, "I know you're used to doing this, Mom, but it upsets me when you make plans for me now. I promise to clear it with you when I'm making plans to go to someone's house if you promise you won't make plans for me without asking. OK?"

What we are talking about here is trying to make others see us differently: more capable, more intelligent, able to make decisions, and needing more freedom. It *can* be done, but the process may be slower than you like. After all, your parents have treated you one way for eleven, twelve, thirteen years. They'll need a chance to shift gears. (Older people don't change as quickly as young people, but they're not hopeless!)

Start by taking the following Image Test. Your answers may help you see yourself as others see you.

IMAGE TEST

Y N

1. __ __ Do I expect an adult to get me up on school mornings and then keep track of when I am supposed to be ready to leave?

2. __ __ Do I make my own lunch for school?

3. __ __ Do I expect Mom or Dad to do my homework or projects?

4. __ __ If I put an assignment off until the last minute, do I expect help in order to get it done?

5. __ __ If I goof up, do I look around for someone else to blame?

6. __ __ Do I perform regular chores around the house without being nagged?

7. __ __ Do I ever offer to help someone else do a job?

8. __ __ Do I whine or throw a tantrum if I don't get my way?

9. __ __ Do I spend my money on fun but throw-away stuff and then have to beg for money for something I really want or need?

10. __ __ Do I ever pay a compliment when some family

member does something well or looks particularly nice?

11. __ __ When I am told to be home at a certain time, do I usually run late, but have an explanation?

12. __ __ Have I ever just walked away from a fight with my sibling and said, "Let's not fight"?

Scoring: Give yourself ten points for every answer that matches: 1. No 2. Yes 3. No 4. No 5. No 6. Yes 7. Yes 8. No 9. No 10. Yes 11. No 12. Yes.

If you got a score of 100 or better, then you probably don't have much of a problem trying to prove that you are responsible, capable, and deserving of more adult treatment. If you scored seventy to ninety, you have a good start! A score of sixty or below and I think you see where you need improvement in order to change your image. Take a Positive Risk and work on those!

Not only is our image important to us during the adolescent years, but our need for privacy becomes greater. This can lead to conflict.

Privacy, Please!

I admit it. I was insensitive. I thought I would surprise my sixteen-year-old sister with an old family photograph, blown up to poster size, for her birthday. Of course, the photo I, her slightly older sister, selected was the one of her standing naked in the birdbath in our front yard when she was only two. I thought it was a funny picture. There she was, in all her naked glory, clutching the statue that was poised in the middle of the birdbath, her hair all soaped up and sticking off the top of her head.

When I made a big show of presenting it to her, all of her friends thought it was funny and laughed too. In fact, they howled. My sister, however, turned bright red, snatched the poster away, and has sworn to this day never to tell anyone where it is. (Personally, I think she tore it up into tiny little pieces and flushed it down the toilet!)

I didn't intend to embarrass her. Not really. But I didn't imagine just how humiliated she would be. I had invaded her privacy and exposed her to the laughter of her friends.

Privacy becomes very important during our adolescent years,

in a way that it never was before, and maybe never will be again. It is the acknowledgment that you are a separate person, deserving of some respect. It is a bit of shelter from the prying eyes of the rest of the world as you change and develop. And privacy gives you some control during a time when you may feel you have very limited control over your life.

Again, it is sometimes a real challenge to remind others in the family that you are now a person in need of some privacy; that you are no longer the little kid they remember, who ran giggling down the block wearing only your favorite yellow socks and a big smile!

"My family will *usually* knock on my bedroom door before coming in, but if they can listen in on my telephone conversations —they will!" said fourteen-year-old Sara.

"I guess I'm lucky because my parents always knock and if I tell them to leave, they do," said Gordon, twelve.

"I don't get any privacy," complained thirteen-year-old John. "If my door is closed, or I'm in the bathroom, my parents may not come in but they stand in the hall asking me questions. If I want any privacy, I have to go for a walk."

Two-thirds of the adolescents I surveyed feel they at least have one room in the house where they can get some privacy. Most said that their bedrooms were their private place, while some mentioned the bathroom or even the basement. If you are in that one-third who don't feel their privacy is respected, what can you do? Bring out the secret weapons!

First, Do a Reality Check. Was your privacy invaded one time or perhaps by accident, or is it a usual practice to: A. Open your mail, B. Walk into your room without asking, or C. Listen in on your telephone conversations?

Identify your feeling and your needs. For example, "It makes me feel angry when someone just walks into my room without knocking. I need for my family members to knock."

Second, remember Cool Communication. Look at the difference in these two dialogues between Becka and her mother.

Becka: "You always walk into my room without knocking. I hate it! I deserve a little respect around here!"
Mother: "Oh yeah? Just remember who owns this house, young lady! This is my house and I'll walk into any room I please, when I

please! Just respect that!"

Now if Becka had used her Secret Weapons, the conversation might have gone like this:

Becka: "Mom, when you walk into my room without knocking, it annoys me. I need a space that I can feel is mine and where I can go to be totally alone to think." (Feeling and need expressed. No attack was made.)
Mother: "You're right, Becka. I know how you feel. If the door to your room is closed, I'll knock. Would that satisfy you?" (Since Mother is not attacked, she can focus on Becka's need.)

Even if your family knocks on your door, leaves your mail alone, and lets you speak to your friends in private, they may sometimes expose you in other ways.

Please Don't Embarrass Me!

"I'll never forget it as long as I live," said Karen, still cringing at the thought. "My mom and I went out to buy my first bra. I was a little embarrassed, and trying to figure out what size I needed was a little embarrassing too. Just as I was looking through the boxes, my little brother, who I thought was shopping with my dad in a different part of the store, yelled out at the top of his lungs from about three aisles away 'How about this one Karen?' On his head he was wearing this *huge* bra. It must have been a 48D or something because he was wearing it like a hat and he looked like Mickey Mouse. Everybody started laughing at him, which only made him scream it again at me and start to follow me around. I wanted to die!"

Being exposed and singled out for attention when you don't want it can be very embarrassing. It is natural, as you are going through many changes, to want to blend in with the crowd until you get your bearings and your confidence level up. If this incident happened to Karen when she was twenty, she probably would have laughed it off, realizing how funny her brother looked. But because she was dealing with an unfamiliar situation involving her changing body, she was embarrassed that the attention was directed her way.

"I hate it when my mother sings to the radio in the car, in front of my friends," said Tommy, twelve. "It is so embarrassing. All my friends look at her and laugh and I just know they're thinking what a jerk I am. Why can't she just be quiet like other mothers and drive?"

"My dad is in a wheelchair," said Bart, thirteen. "When he doesn't like something my friends are saying or doing, he won't say anything to them but as he passes, he'll roll over their toes with his wheelchair. It's so embarrassing!"

"With me, it's my brothers who embarrass me all the time," said fourteen-year-old Betsy. "I'm the youngest of five children and the only girl. Every time I get a telephone call, if any of my brothers answers it, they'll ask in a loud voice 'Who is this guy? Isn't he the one you have such a big crush on, Betsy?' or 'Isn't this the guy you said was such a dork, Betsy?' It's so embarrassing."

In each of these cases, the secret weapons may be used to try to prevent any more embarrassments.

Tommy has a couple of ways to proceed. He can Do a Reality Check by asking his friends if *their* parents ever sing in the car. He might find that they do. In that case, he and his friends can agree that parents are a little nuts and just smile when the singing fills the car. Option two is to decide that he would really like his mother *not* to sing in front of his friends but he'll have to Take a Positive Risk and offer an alternative. Using Cool Communication, he might approach his mother and say, "Mom, I know you love to sing and I don't mind listening to you, but when you sing to the radio in front of my friends I feel embarrassed. Do you think that you can sing when we are alone in the car, but when my friends are there you can just drive and talk?" This is a much cooler approach than "You always embarrass me in the car in front of my friends. Don't sing. Just don't sing!"

Bart also has to communicate his feelings to his dad about rolling over his friends' toes. He might try: "Can we talk about this, Dad? If my friends do or say something to upset you, maybe you can just give me a signal or tell them to stop. It embarrasses me when you roll over their toes."

Betsy may need to call a family meeting to communicate her feelings to her brothers. Perhaps they don't realize that their constant teasing upsets her and makes the other person on the line embarrassed as well. Then again, maybe they do and they tease her anyway. In that case Betsy may need to say, "It makes me angry and upset that you don't treat me with the same kind of respect that you feel you need. How can we change this?" By forcing her brothers to come up with a solution, Betsy is halfway there to solving her problem without name-calling and screaming.

But even the best intentions and the coolest communicators fall apart once in a while. That's when the real fighting starts!

CHAPTER 3

FiɢHTiNɢ?
WHO'S FiɢHTiNɢ?

Imagine that you are a bird. It's a warm spring day and you decide to fly from house to house to see what the humans are doing. The first windowsill you land on has a mother yelling to her fourteen-year-old son.

"Tim, come empty the garbage. Everything's falling out of the bag and onto the floor."

"I'll do it later, Mom," yells Tim. "I'm watching TV."

"You always say that and it doesn't get done. Do it now!"

As Tim yells something back, you fly away. Too noisy at that house. Let's go to the next. A mother and her twelve-year-old daughter are facing each other down in the living room.

"I can't stand this!" yells the mother. "If I say the sky is blue, you say it's green! Can't you stop fighting and just agree? What's the matter with you?"

"I'm just telling you what I think. I don't have to agree with everything you say just because *you* say it!" yells the daughter. "Why don't you ever ask for my opinion instead of just telling me what to do and think?"

Another noisy house! Let's fly to one more windowsill and see if anyone is going to enjoy this beautiful day. Ah, there are a couple of kids playing in the front yard. Upstairs a window is opening and a girl is poking her head out.

"You little creeps!" she screams at the kids in the yard. "I've told you never to come into my room! You messed up my tapes and took my candy! I hate you! I'm gonna tell Dad to beat you up!"

Whew! Enough of humans! Isn't anyone having a quiet time?

Probably not, if there's an adolescent in the house. Not only is this period a time of change and growth, it is also a constant struggle, a struggle for territory (your room), for independence (making your own decisions), and for recognition that you are becoming a whole, thinking person separate from your parents.

This is all very normal, but the hard part is that it takes you, and everyone close to you, some time to adjust to the person you are becoming. You may know that you have changed inside, but the rest of the world around you (remember, nobody's a mind reader!) needs some proof first. Struggles can be pretty noisy, but with a secret weapon and a different approach, conflicts can be an opportunity for you to grow and learn rather than pull your family apart.

WHO'S GOT THE POWER?

Bobby, at thirteen, is the oldest of three children. He's a good student in school, has been respectful of his parents and other adults, and usually tries to get along. Lately, though, he and his parents have been having a lot of fights, particularly on the weekend.

"Every Sunday our whole family goes to my grandparents' house for dinner and it's always the same. It's boring. I either wind up having to baby-sit all the littler kids while the adults talk or I'm left out because I don't fit into any age group. I don't want to go. Why do I always have to go with them everywhere? I'd rather stay home and practice my guitar or play a computer game and relax," he says.

One of the toughest things about being this age is that you have a lot of developing interests, yet your time is usually controlled by other people. You may be fighting about going to your grandparents, going to the movies, or going shopping with your family but what you are really struggling for is control.

Face it, while you are a minor, living in your parents' house, *they* are the ones with the control, but that doesn't mean you can't present options and try to negotiate a more agreeable situation for yourself. Remember, a person who listens and communicates has power. A child who whines and yells has no power.

First, Do a Reality Check of the situation. Your parents expect you to go to Grandma's every Sunday. You *feel* bored and sometimes left out. You *need* to do something fun and interesting with your Sunday.

What options can you Coolly Communicate to your parents?

Perhaps they'll let you include a close friend in the family gathering. Or you might take your guitar, computer disks, or video with you. Better yet, why not offer to play cameraman and make a video of Sunday At Grandma's, interviewing all the relatives. Not only would it be fun but it might become a family treasure — thanks to you.

Another set of options might include being allowed to skip one Sunday a month to do something else. Think! Brainstorm! You *can* have some control over your time if you approach the problem in a more mature manner.

Another major battleground is the doing of chores around the house. Tim, at the beginning of the chapter, whose mother wanted him to empty the garbage, might avoid a fight if he proceeded like this:

Mother: "Tim, come empty the garbage. Everything's falling out of the bag and onto the floor!"
Tim: "Mom, my show is at a really good part but a commercial is coming up. I promise to empty it at the commercial, OK?"
Mother: "OK."

Then Tim had better keep his end of the bargain or he will not have his mother's trust that he will keep his word in the future. This type of option-offer will work for most situations where a parent is dictating and you might feel like rebelling. Offering an option and communicating that option in a cool fashion will give you some measure of control and show your parents that you are, indeed, growing up and are more capable than they thought.

Bedtime Bashing

The word "bedtime" went off like a bomb in the middle of the room. Everyone in the classroom had a bedtime argument to make.

"It's not fair," said Danny, eleven. "When I was eight, I had to go to bed at eight o'clock. My little sister is eight and she stays up until 8:30, which is the same time I go to bed now!"

"Yeah, I think I should get to stay up later, too," said Tina. "All the good TV shows go on at nine o'clock and most of my friends get to see them. I try to tell my parents that I can get up in the morning but we wind up fighting about it."

"I'm the youngest one in my family and I do get to stay up late," said Todd, looking at Danny. "My problem is my older brother and sister start yelling because they had to go to bed earlier, so they get mad at me."

Bedtimes are touchy subjects. A later bedtime is viewed as a mark of growing up, so naturally it often becomes the subject of a family fight. But let's Do a Reality Check. What do you really want out of the situation? Do you just want to stay up later, whether it's in front of the TV or in your room? Is there a specific television program you want to see on a regular basis?

Now listen to your parents' arguments against your later bedtime. Listening is a very important part of disagreeing with someone because it will give you a hint of what's really going on. If you are only concentrating on what you want to say, you may miss a point that will help you win an argument.

For example, you want to stay up an hour later and your parents say no "because you are too young." They might mean they are concerned that you could not cope with the later hour and still be alert for school in the morning.

If they say no because "it's just too late for you to be up," they may mean that they need a little private and quiet time too. (After all, they are entitled to it.) Both of these cases assume that your request is reasonable.

So, *listen* to your parents' objections and then present options. If it is one show that you want to watch, communicate that. If your parents want some quiet time to themselves, you may be able to compromise and stay up an extra half-hour in your room reading or listening to music.

Other suggestions come from adolescents who have been through it themselves. "Instead of whining, say OK and go to bed right away. Then the next day, do a job or something that makes you look more mature," advises Craig, twelve. "Then you have something to show them that makes you look more grown up."

"A contract always works for me when I'm trying to persuade my parents," says Dave, thirteen. "I put in it what I am willing to do in return for the favor I am asking. If I don't live up to my part of the contract, they don't have to live up to theirs."

"If you get good grades, parents ease up on you a lot," says Jen. "I wanted to stay up a half-hour later but they didn't think I could do it and still get good grades. I asked them to let me try the later bedtime for a week. At the end of the week, my quizzes were still good grades, so I got the later bedtime. If my grades slip, though, I'll have to go to bed earlier, so I'm studying harder!"

"Get help from an older brother or sister if you have one," says Ann. "Sometimes it's better to have them argue for you. Of course, you'll probably owe them."

That's great if you can get a brother or sister to help you out, but what if that brother or sister is your major problem?

I Wish I Was an Only Child!

What are the three things you can count on parents to say, practically from the time you're born until the time you leave the nest? "Brush your teeth," "Eat your vegetables," and "Stop fighting!"

"Stop fighting?" you say. "Tell her to stop fighting! *I* wasn't doing anything."

Do you ever wonder whether you will *ever* be friends with your brother or sister? Some of you might answer, "Who'd *want* to be friends?" The truth of the matter is that your sibling will one day become one of the most important people in your life. You may find it difficult to believe now, but one day when you are both much older, it will be your sibling who remembers you as a child when all of those around you only know you as an adult. It will be your sibling who will be able to remember and laugh at a shared memory of your growing up years. It is your sibling who will share your family history and maybe even your looks and personality traits.

Fine for the future, you say, but how does that keep him out of my things now?

"Having a sister can be a pain," said Ty, fourteen. "Parents are together because they love each other and decided to get married. Brothers and sisters didn't have a choice. You have to learn to get used to each other and to love each other and sometimes, that's not real easy!"

Beth, eleven, agrees. "Vacations and trips are the worst! You're stuck together all of the time. Usually you have to share a car seat, a room, or even a bed. I'd rather sleep on the floor! They take your things and try to get you in trouble and if my little brother hits me, I can't hit him back because my parents say I'm older and should know better!"

"I hate it when my older sister comes into my room and touches or takes my things," said Rene. "Just because she's older, she thinks she rules the house and can touch my stuff. It makes me really mad."

No doubt about it, brothers and sisters can complicate your peaceful life. They can poke you or deliberately step on your toes as they pass and swipe the cookie off your plate and then look like angels if you yell for Mom or Dad to step in. I'll never forget one car trip that I took with my parents and two younger sisters when we actually fought over who was looking out whose window and breathing whose air! It was then that we learned to duck the arm that quickly stretched out from the front seat and tried to smack any kid in the way!

So what can you do? It doesn't take a Reality Check to realize that you probably aren't going to be able to change your sibling's behavior. The only thing you can change is how you react to any given situation. After all, if what you are trying to prove is that you are no longer a child, you blow your argument if you wind up screaming your lungs out while you punch out your little brother for sneaking into your room, right? Let's take a look at a few of the more common sibling conflicts.

Problem: *Your sibling keeps sneaking into your bedroom and taking things without your permission.*

Solution: First, Do a Reality Check. Your room is your private territory, with your private things where you can dream and play. You want to keep siblings out . . . but it's the first place you take a friend and lock the door. You need control. Siblings may want your attention and be jealous of your friends.

Options: If it is a younger sibling, you can try inviting him into your room for a limited time so he can satisfy his curiosity and feel important that his big sister or brother is paying attention to him. If it is an older sibling, Cool Communication may get the point across that you expect the same privacy and respect that he does.

Problem: *Your sibling seems to control the television remote control,* *even to the point of hiding it when she leaves the room. And she always get her way in watching whatever television show she wants.*

Solution: Do a Reality Check. Do you ever get control of the television? Do you stay up later and get to watch more shows than your sibling? If there is unequal treatment, then Cool Communication to your parents is needed.

Remember to present options — don't just complain. For example: "How about if Cindy and I look at the TV listing at the beginning of the week and each pick three shows that we really want to see." That way, when the day comes, there's no fighting. Other options include dividing the control by hours or alternate days. Just keep in mind that you're not always going to win — and that's part of the Reality Check too. You win some and lose some. That's life!

Problem: *A brother or sister makes you look bad in front of your friends by teasing, calling names, or just being a pest.*

Solution: A Reality Check of this situation will show you that your brother or sister is trying to get your attention in a very juvenile way. That doesn't make it acceptable and that's what you have to let her know. Instead of screaming "You jerk! Leave us alone!" it might be more effective if you present an option. "Leave Charlie and me alone and I'll play Mike Tyson's Punch Out with you when he leaves."

The list of things that brothers and sisters fight over is as long and varied as brothers and sisters themselves. It can go on and on: pets, chores, music, the front seat of the car, movies, foods ... you name it! While some of the fights take you by surprise, you pretty much know which things you are going to wind up fighting over ... after all, you've fought over them before. Next time, surprise everyone and be prepared. You might even surprise yourself!

CHAPTER 4

Cake Mixes Blend – Not People!

Debby's parents got divorced when she was eight years old. She lived with her mom, Mary, and visited her dad every other weekend. Then when she was twelve years old, her mom married again. Bob, the man she had met at a business conference and fallen in love with, had been married before but his wife had died. He had a fourteen-year-old son who lived with them. So the new family consisted of Debby's mom, her stepfather, her stepbrother Mike, and herself.

When Debby's mom married Bob, it meant that they had to move from their little apartment in Maryland to a ranch in Texas. Bob was a nice man and he felt family was very important. He cared about Debby and wanted her and his son to be happy in the new family. Debby was going to get her own room and her own horse. It sounds as though Debby and her new family were going to live happily ever after, doesn't it?

By the end of the first year, Debby threatened to run away from home. By the end of the second year, she had gotten into trouble with the police. By the third year, her new family was on the verge of breaking up. What happened?

When Debby's mom and Bob married, their new family became what is being called today a "blended family." That is, a new family made up of two others who have gone through divorce or the loss of a parent. It might be called a blended family or a stepfamily, but whichever term is used, certain government estimates claim that 1,300 stepfamilies, with children, are being formed *every day*! One out of every three adolescents lives in some form of stepfamily. In fact, some experts say that if divorce rates continue as they are now, by the end of this century, the stepfamily, or blended family, will be the largest type of single family in the country! That's a lot of stepfamilies!

If those of you in a more traditional family face stresses and frustrations as you make that charge towards adulthood, those in a stepfamily face even more complicated stresses. Very often the fact that you are going through adolescence (a separation from your family) and becoming part of a stepfamily actually work against each other. There are new people to deal with, new rules, new feelings, and maybe even a new address.

Is it possible to deal with these changes successfully? Yes, if you use the secret weapons. Let's take a look at some of the special problems you might face if you were becoming part of a stepfamily.

I Want to Go Home!

Debby had been in Texas for only two months when she felt she had the worst day of her life! She hadn't made any real friends in her new seventh grade and missed her friends she had known since kindergarten. She felt one of her teachers didn't like her and the work level was different from her other school. When she went into the lunchroom, she thought Mike and his friends were laughing at her and she was convinced when he turned his back on her. She was miserable! When she got off the bus after a long, dusty ride out to the ranch, she threw herself in her mother's arms. "I want to go home!" she cried. "I miss Dad and my friends and my little room. Nobody likes me. I hate it here!"

Naturally Debby's mother was upset and later that night, Bob was upset. After all, he was doing everything he could to make her happy. It wound up being a big family fight with even Mike calling her an ungrateful brat.

It's hard to move away from friends at any time, but for a young person in a new stepfamily, it may also mean moving away from a biological parent. Where before, Debby was able to visit her father every other weekend, she was only going to be able to visit him on holidays and vacations while she lived in Texas.

Also, Debby was feeling so sorry for herself, that she hadn't really tried to make friends in her new home. If she had Done a Reality Check of the situation she might have found this: she is part of a new family and her new home is Texas. She misses her father and *feels* sad. She misses her friends and all the familiar places she was used to. She *needs* friends with whom she can hang around, talk on the telephone, and share confidences. She *needs* to see her father.

Now what could she do? Options: Communicate those specific feelings and needs to her mom and Bob. They are probably trying their best to make her happy but they are not mind readers. Perhaps an arrangement can be made where Debby can fly home for a weekend or her dad could fly out. She could telephone her old friends or even send a video of her new home. It is important to keep up old friendships as you make the change to new ones.

In order to make friends, Debby would also have to take charge. She could invite a couple of girls out to her new home. She could join a club at school. She was always a good tennis player so maybe she could join a tennis team. She really has more control of her situation than she realizes. But there are other parts of the situation that she needs to take a look at as well.

LEAVE ME ALONE!

Just as Debby's mom and Bob began working very hard to form a new family, Debby was going through her adolescent period of separation. Instead of joining the family after dinner to watch television or go for a walk, she opted to stay in her room to listen to music. When Bob suggested a weekend campout or fishing trip for the family, Debby said she'd rather ride her horse. When she wanted to talk to just her mom, Bob always seemed to be around. And when she suggested to her mom that just the two of them go on a shopping trip, her mom wanted to include Bob. This led to more arguing.

Bob and Debby's mother had their feelings hurt and felt Debby was rejecting the new family — she seemed to lock herself away from them whenever possible. Debby was angry that, after having her mother all to herself for four years, she now had to share her with Bob and Mike.

Quick, Do a Reality Check! Bob and Mary are working to strengthen a new marriage and family relationship. Debby is doing what adolescents normally do — separate from the family. You can see how these two situations work against each other and could cause hurt feelings on both sides. The same kind of situation is going on down the road in other families, but because they aren't involved in trying to make a stepfamily work, it's not thought of as rejection.

Also, Debby was feeling jealous of Bob and Mike and the attention her mother was giving them. What she *needed* was a little bit of alone time with her mom. What are the options? Debby could Coolly Communicate those feelings. "I love you, Mom and Bob, but I need time alone. I'm not rejecting you. I'm just growing up. I also need some time with just my mom. In return, I will make an effort to participate in some family activities."

OK, so Debby started spending more time with the new family. But everything wasn't happy yet. In fact, it seemed to create even more problems!

Whose Rules Are These, Anyway?

Did you ever stop to think about the rules your family follows every day? For example, do you all sit down to dinner together? Do you say grace? Are there certain foods you all eat with your fingers? Are there certain rules about telephone calls during meals or on school nights? And how about weekends and special days? Are you allowed to have a friend sleep over? If you get a good report card, is there a special reward?

Since our family customs and rules are in effect from the time we are little, we take them for granted. They are part of life. But not everyone does things the same way. Different families have different ways of doing even the simplest of things.

These differences can become very real problems when a divorce and remarriage occurs. In fact, there is even one more factor to complicate things.

Between the time that a divorce or death of a parent occurs and a remarriage takes place, a single-parent family exists. Very often, many of the regular family rules you lived by are relaxed a little to accommodate a tired, working parent and new situation. Then a remarriage occurs and a stepfamily is formed. What happens? You have two sets of family rules that crash right into each other!

Debby ran into a number of these clashes and they caused a lot of arguments. For example:

Debby and her mom had gotten used to eating dinner off snack trays in front of the television set. Bob wanted the family to sit down at the table for a regular dinnertime.

Debby was used to being able to talk with friends on the telephone after school. Bob and Mike had a rule that telephone conversations on school nights were limited to homework questions and/or ten minutes.

Both Mike and Debby were used to receiving an allowance but Mike was expected to buy his school lunches, pay for dates, and buy some of his own clothes with his allowance. Exceptions were heavy coats or suits. Debby, on the other hand, was given an allowance to be spent on frivolous things. She had depended on her mother to buy her clothes and give her money daily for school lunches and outings.

You can see where these differences within one new family could cause problems. A Reality Check of the situation makes it obvious that a family needs to operate on a single set of rules and those rules should be agreed upon by all members. A family meeting is needed to present the problems and Coolly Communicate the options. Perhaps a compromise can be struck somewhere in between. For example: The family sits down to dinner together every day of the week except Friday or Saturday, when members might have separate social plans. Those staying at home can eat in front of the television on a snack tray.

The point is, name-calling and hurt feelings will not make the differences go away. Remember that the power is in communication and the one who communicates is able to take charge.

Not only are household rules undergoing a change in a stepfamily, but even your place in the family may shift. This could leave you wondering "Where do I fit in?" all over again.

From Oldest to Youngest in a Flash!

Debby had been an only child in her original family. Mike had been an only child in his original family. Now, in the new family, Mike found himself the oldest and Debby found herself the youngest. Both those positions made them feel uneasy.

"I keep feeling like I'm supposed to be looking out for her all the time," says Mike. "I'm not used to it. She's big enough to take care of herself. What does she need from me?"

At the same time, Debby began to resent having someone else tell her what to do. "I can make my own decisions about friends," she said angrily. "What right does Mike have to tell me that I'm hanging around with the wrong kinds of people? He's not my real brother anyway! Let him mind his own business!"

In addition to trying to figure out how to relate to each other in the family, Debby resented the privileges that Mike got just because he was two years older than she was. He received a larger allowance, a later bedtime, and more freedom to go off with his friends.

Mike, on the other hand, resented the expensive presents that Debby received from her biological father — the miniature television, the stereo, the designer clothes, and the extra cash he sent her with his letters. And while he had to spend the holidays with his Dad and new stepmother, Debby was flown to the Bahamas to spend the holidays with her dad.

This inequality is a very real part of life in a stepfamily that "blends" two sets of kids. It is part of the Reality Check. At a time of life when you are becoming very conscious of fairness and equal treatment, this reality may seem totally unacceptable. There are options, however.

The first is to accept that this is going to be a part of life and recognize your feelings towards it. Mike could express "It makes me angry that Debby gets to go on special trips and I have to stay here at home." His feelings can then be dealt with and that's much more productive than simply screaming, "I hate Debby!"

Another option might be to let Debby's dad know how his unequal treatment is causing trouble for Debby, so that he tones down his gifts. Since divorced parents are not often in a mood to cooperate, however, it might be better if either Debby herself or another member of the family, besides her mother, suggests this.

Unequal treatment because of the new place held in the family circle is going to have to be dealt with in a realistic way as well. Whether your position has shifted to oldest, youngest, or middle, the new position carries both privileges and responsibilities. Debby may not be able to stay up as late as Mike, but Mike also has to do chores that Debby doesn't have to do. By focusing on the positives of your new position, it will be easier to accept or change the realities of those points you don't like.

Over the course of the first year, Debby and Mike had another problem to face that neither one expected. That was their feelings for each other.

CRUSHES AND CURSES

Debby woke up one day to find that she had a crush on Mike, her stepbrother. Of course, it didn't happen overnight. It had been developing for a while. Her body was changing, hormones were racing through her body and Mike was ... well, there. He was good looking, he was nice for the most part, and he was popular in school. Debby was very confused. She knew that romantic feelings between brothers and sisters were considered wrong, but Mike wasn't her real brother. She didn't dare tell her mother or Bob because she was afraid they would be shocked and angry with her.

Mike, for his part, was having a problem, too. He had noticed Debby's developing breasts and figure and when the braces came off her teeth, she was really pretty! He too had some romantic feelings for her but was also confused by these feelings that he knew, in his head, that he should not have. He dealt with it the only way he knew how — he ignored Debby. Mike figured that if he didn't come in contact with her, he wouldn't have to deal with his feelings. There were many times that Debby tried to talk to him and he just said something nasty and brushed her off. He was afraid to get too close, because he really didn't know how to act.

Debby and Mike wound up fighting all the time. Debby was trying to get Mike's attention and Mike was trying to stay away from her. This was all because they didn't know how to deal with the new romantic feelings towards each other.

What Debby and Mike were feeling was very common and perfectly normal. It *is* confusing, though, when you find you may have romantic feelings for a member of your new family. But *feelings* are not right or wrong. *Actions* can be right or wrong, but there is a big difference between *feeling* something and *doing* something.

Between the time your body begins its transformation from child to adult and the time your emotional maturity catches up to your body (usually in the late teens), you will have romantic feelings for many people. That's such a wonderful part of growing up and developing. It helps us sort out what we truly like about a member of the opposite sex, how we can relate to them, and how we can make relationships work. It is a preparation for finally choosing a mate.

When this occurs in a stepfamily, however, it presents some very special problems. Let's see what happens if Debby and Mike used the secret weapons to deal with this confusing situation.

A Reality Check would show that Debby and Mike are attracted to each other in a romantic and perhaps physical sense. They are not just two individuals, but stepbrother and stepsister. If they were to indulge in a romantic relationship, it might be fun for awhile but it would probably fade and end as they find others whom they develop romantic feelings towards. When the romantic relationship fades, they still have to live together as stepbrother and stepsister. This could be very difficult, at best. At its worst, it could break up the family.

What are the options? Debby and Mike could sit down and talk and Coolly Communicate their feelings towards each other as well as take a look at the reality of the situation. They could agree that the best course of action would be to view each other as special friends, but off-limits for romantic involvement. They could agree to set down some ground rules for their behavior towards each other so as not to make the other person feel uncomfortable. These could include being affectionate but not kissing each other on the lips, not running around in their underwear, and granting each other the same kind of privacy both at home and in outside friendships that they would expect of a "regular" sibling.

Having a crush on a new stepbrother or stepsister is not wrong. It is not unnatural, but acting upon those feelings could be hurtful and lead to some very difficult problems within the family. It is important to look beyond the immediate desire to the consequences of your actions and figure out if they are worth the trouble. After Doing a Reality Check, identifying your feelings and needs, and looking at your options, you will discover a much better long-term solution to your situation.

CHAPTER 5

GRANDPA IS MOVING IN?

Thirteen-year-old Jason and his two younger brothers were really excited when his parents told them that their Grandpa Fred was going to come live with them. Grandpa Fred was one of Jason's favorite people in the whole world!

Grandpa's hobby was magic and Jason had seen him perform for both kids and adults. He never failed to teach Jason a new trick when the two of them were together. Jason had heard his parents talking about how Grandpa Fred was kind of sick, not quite himself anymore, and very lonely since Grandma died four years ago, but Jason was sure that he and his brothers and Grandpa would have a great time together! Imagine all the magic tricks they could learn!

It did not work out quite the way Jason thought it would.

Grandpa slept a lot during the day and would get very angry if Jason and his brothers made noise after school. Sometimes, when Jason had a friend over, Grandpa would embarrass him by passing gas or burping or making other noises without even saying "Excuse me." And all Grandpa seemed to do was criticize Jason—his haircut, his clothes, his attitude, and his friends. When Grandpa answered the telephone and found out it was a friend of Jason's whom he didn't like and hung up on him, Jason exploded and screamed "I wish you had never moved in here!"

What comes to mind when you think of *your* grandparents? Walks in the park? Homemade cookies? Stories from days past? Now how would you feel about one of your grandparents moving into your house permanently?

When it comes to family, our country has gone through many changes. Up until the 1950s, it was not unusual for several generations of family members to live either together or in the same neighborhood. Over the last thirty years, families were split up due to job transfers and better methods of transportation. Now we are once more in a period of change. Senior citizens are living longer due to better health care, but because of the high cost of living, it is expensive for them to live on their own.

So once again, it is becoming more common for a grandparent, or even an elderly aunt or uncle, to move in with younger family members. Having several generations of a family under one roof can be a tremendous experience. It can also create some stresses that need to be recognized and dealt with.

Getting the Word

"Nobody asked me anything," said Eileen, eleven, crossly. "It's as though I didn't even count! I'm a member of the family, too, but I didn't even know that my grandmother was moving in until the week before it happened! That's when they told me I was going to have to share my room with her because I'm the youngest. It's not fair!"

It's tough to have a new person join the family circle even if that person is a relative already. It means giving up a little more privacy, a little more of your parents' time, and maybe even your own private space—your room! At a time when you feel you have little control over your life, you may tend to view the addition of another adult to the family as just one more person who will be there to tell you what to do! Or you may view a grandparent moving in as the addition of a playmate who will be a constant source of fun whenever you decide to tap into it. Both are unrealistic pictures of the situation, so begin by Doing a Reality Check.

In an ideal situation, the decision to have a grandparent move into your home should be discussed by the whole family — including the grandparent. It is a decision that will affect every member of the family and each member is sure to have some concerns. While you are focusing on how your freedom may be more limited, your grandparent may be feeling the same thing. After all, here is an adult who has raised a family and been independent for a long time, and is now suddenly looking at moving in with a young family once more. This means a loss of privacy for this person as well, and being surrounded by unfamiliar noise, music, and people at a time of life when he or she might just want peace and quiet.

"We had a family meeting to talk about my grandmother

moving in," said Bonnie, twelve. "I think my parents had already made the decision but it was good for us kids to be able to say what we thought about it. I had a lot of questions because my grandmother needs a part-time nurse and I didn't know if I was going to have to help nurse her or what. I always felt a little nervous around really sick people because I don't know what to say. I talked to my parents about that and boy, was I glad to find out that a nurse would still be helping out. Now I've learned to help some too and I don't feel as nervous around sick people."

By Doing a Reality Check and identifying your feelings about the situation, you can communicate those feelings to your parents and grandparent at a time when an emotional battle isn't going on. It's much easier to be prepared for a possible problem than to blow up in the middle of a situation.

If the decision has been made and grandpa or grandma is moving in, then living together can be an adventure.

Living Together

"Ever since my grandmother moved in, I get two opinions on everything I do," said Katie, thirteen.

"Having my grandmother live with us means I have an extra mother to nag on me," said Russell, twelve.

"My grandfather contradicts privileges and other things that my parents say," said Jean, fourteen.

Complaints, complaints, complaints! Who was this person who moved in with you — your grandparent or Count Dracula? Some aren't quite sure. Of the hundreds of kids I've talked to for this book, about one out of every fifteen had a grandparent living with them either permanently or temporarily. They agree that this kind of living arrangement has added a new word to their vocabulary — tolerance!

When we think of the word tolerance, we might think of having sympathy for, and accepting people of a different race, religion, or color. This sounds very honorable. When it comes to tolerance within our own families, however, it becomes tougher to practice. It may be easy to see past a schoolmate's different color and religion to the person underneath, but when it comes to having to listen to Grandpa's World War II story for the eighty-seventh time, suddenly our ears snap shut, our patience runs out, and our feet head for a different room.

"It's bad enough I have to put up with a little brother but now I have to live with my grandfather, too," said Jessica. "The only television programs the two of them watch are sports, sports, sports. I can't stand it! Nobody ever takes my side anymore!"

What would happen if Jessica did a Reality Check? She might find that she is *feeling* left out and what she *needs* is a turn to express her preferences; maybe even some special time with her mother doing "girl" type things. Looking at options might include taking turns with the television programming or even getting her grandfather interested in something that holds her interest. Then these can be Coolly Communicated. Jessica might find, through communication, that her grandfather is watching sports with her little brother because he is also feeling left out and that's a way for him to have company!

Situations such as Jean's and Russell's call for good communication among family members too. Very often, when a grandparent moves in, they do so with the feeling that they are going to "help out" in the family. Part of this helping out means that they will help watch over you. They genuinely care about you — you already know that. But suddenly, they have gone from being wonderful Grandma or Grandpa who was there for fun stuff to being ... well, another parent — just when you may feel you're having difficulty dealing with the ones you have!

"I can't even get away with sneaking outside without a coat or socks," said Russell. "If my mother doesn't catch me, my grandmother does and then I get the lecture about when Uncle Jack got pneumonia!"

Jean's grandfather was only trying to help out, too, when he contradicted certain privileges that she felt she had. "He doesn't let me stay on the telephone longer than thirty seconds!" says Jean. "He says I ought to be studying. But my parents let me talk on the phone as long as my homework is done. I hate having to take orders from so many people!"

A Reality Check of Jean's situation shows that her grandfather, who has recently moved in, is not aware of all the house rules yet.

He is trying to look out for Jean and be helpful. Jean is *feeling* confused and angry that she is being given two contradictory rules to obey. An option is for the entire family to sit down and discuss the rules of the house so everyone is working under the same set. Remember that communicating feelings lets other people know what's going on inside your head without attacking them. That leaves you all free to work on the *problem*, not the *attack*!

Far from being all problems, there are many positive sides to having a grandparent move in.

I've Found a Special Friend!

"My grandmother's great!" said Linda. "I'd rather talk to her than to my mom because my mom criticizes and my grandmother really listens!"

"I like having my grandmother live with us," said Kevin. "When I have good news or I've done well in school, she makes a bigger deal out of it than my parents and that makes me feel really special."

"There are four kids in my family and both my parents work," said Carla, fifteen. "My grandma is the one who's home when we get home from school and she always has milk and cookies or muffins or something special waiting for us. She said she used to do it for my mom so she's doing it for us, too!"

Yes, it can be a real treat having a grandparent live with you, even if it's different than what you may have first expected. Just think — your grandmother is not having difficulty separating from you as you grow to adulthood because she is not your parent. Your grandfather has years of experience and advice *and* he knows your family. That puts your grandparent in the ideal position to be your very special friend!

"I used to think my grandmother was so old-fashioned until I started telling her about some trouble I was having with a friend at school," said Margaret. "It turns out that she had the same kind of problem when she was my age and she gave me good advice. My mother doesn't like this friend so I didn't really want to tell her what was going on. She would have said 'dump her' and I probably would have gotten mad even though I know she just cares about me. She would have gotten emotional and Grandma just told me a story. I'm glad she was there."

Having a grandparent in the house can be a surprise in other ways as well. Mindy, eleven, started a stitching club at school because her grandmother taught her and her friends how to embroider — something her lawyer mother never enjoyed. Mark, twelve, has gotten into woodworking with his grandfather. This year he plans to make all of his own Christmas gifts for family members. And Aaron is slowly learning German — the language his grandfather grew up speaking.

Our grandparents are our links to the past. We are their links to the future. We can make those links strong if we use the three secret weapons to overcome those challenges of living together.

PART TWO

YOU AND YOUR FRIENDS

CHAPTER 6

I Thought We Were Friends!

There is an old Beatles song that says "You Gotta Have Friends." It was popular when it came out and it is still popular today. In fact, it could be an adolescent's theme song because more than ever before or possibly ever again, friends are the important people in your life.

When you were a child, your parents picked your friends for you. Maybe it was because they lived on the same block, you were in daycare together, or your parents were all friends. It didn't really matter. Your friends were probably around the same age and you could play with cars or dolls with one almost as well as another. But now, all that is changing.

Now, *you* pick your friends and the reasons are different, too. Most of those surveyed said that the three top reasons for picking a friend now is someone who is fun, someone who is kind, and someone who can be trusted. That's a little more complicated than just living in the same neighborhood, isn't it? But friendships right now are getting more complicated and their effects on you can change the course of your life!

What are Friends for?

Here are some comments from sixth, seventh, and eighth graders.

"A friend listens to you, no matter what."

"A friend will stick up for you when someone else is picking on you."

"When you get into trouble in school, a friend will get into trouble with you."

"A friend will keep your secrets and not laugh at you when you tell them something that may sound silly but is important to you."

"A friend will have sympathy for you when you are down, even if the reason doesn't sound too important."
"A friend likes me for what I am."

Why do you pick *your* friends? Do you have just one special friend or a number of friends? Do your friends change from week to week? Are your friends known for being fun? cool? kind?

Stop for a minute and think about the people you consider your friends. Now think of how they make you feel about yourself. Being accepted by a group of friends lets you know that you are OK, even though you aren't always sure about yourself, or getting straight A's in school, or even the best looking person in the room.

We tend to hang out with people who share our interests. Are you finding that your friends tend to be those most interested in sports? In music and drama? In dating and relationships?

Everyone needs a support system — that is, a group of people we can rely on for help, sympathy, and fun. It is particularly important during this changing period of your life that your support system reflects what you really need and want. Just like everything else in your life right now, that may change weekly. And sometimes change is hard to deal with because feelings get hurt.

Hey, Who are You Anyway?

Tony and Jim had been best friends since they were in kindergarten. They went trick or treating together, rode together on the school bus, and even stayed over at each others' house on weekends. Suddenly, when they were twelve, everything between them began to change. Jim began hanging around with the kids who appeared to care more about their looks, sports, and calling girls on the telephone than schoolwork and model rockets.

Tony didn't like the changes in his best friend. If that wasn't bad enough, Jim started putting Tony down in front of other people. That really hurt Tony's feelings. First he thought that maybe he did something to make Jim turn away from him. Then Tony just got mad and began to look for other friends. Now he hardly ever talks to Jim anymore.

It hurts when a special friend moves away to another part of the country, but sometimes it hurts even more when a friend changes and moves away emotionally. Change is OK, after all, as long as you are changing together — like going from sixth grade to seventh. But when change comes at different times, or in different ways, it causes conflicts and hurts.

Obviously, we all grow physically at different rates. Just as some get taller than others at around eleven or twelve, bodies, emotions, and interests all progress at different rates as well. This is part of the dynamic change you are going through right now that will not really slow down until your late teens. One week you might be interested in horses, the next week you might be interested in flying planes. One day you are loving a rock group and the next month, you may discover country music. One week you are telling everyone that you want to be a TV star when you grow up and the next, you think that being a professional ballplayer is the way to go. That's great. That's wonderful. That's normal. So why does your friend poop out on you? Why can't he or she share your interests with the same enthusiasm that you shared when you went trick or treating together?

Imagine an apple orchard. You are an apple on one tree and your friend is an apple on the next tree. Because of your positions, you get sun at slightly different times of the day. When it rains, one of you gets slightly more rain and the wind whips through the orchard and blows you around a little more than your friend. Your trees are also slightly different in size. Would you expect both apples to ripen to exactly the same color and size at the same time? Of course not. But we expect that our friends will "ripen" exactly the same as we do and when they don't, it's sometimes viewed as an insult. This unreal *expectation* that we place on our friends often causes conflicts over change.

Time to bring out the secret weapons! If you start with a Reality Check, you will find that you and your friends are ripening at different rates, just like the apples. Unlike the apples, however, you have feelings of wanting to belong and to be accepted. People of all ages cope with change in different ways. Some get scared, some get angry, and some get excited. Tony's friend Jim got a little scared at the changes he was going through. He expected Tony to change with him and when he didn't, he reacted by putting Tony down. It was if he was saying, "If you can't keep up with me, you're just not as good."

What could Tony do? If he used Cool Communication, he could try to sit down and talk to Jim and say "It really hurts my feelings when you put me down, especially when you do it in front of other people." Tony might find that Jim just thought he was being clever or funny or cool. He wasn't looking at it from Tony's point of view that Jim was being mean or being a traitor to their friendship.

Using the third secret weapon, Tony could then Take a Positive Risk by making friends with a number of other people instead of just expecting Jim to stay the same. In fact, because of all the changes that Jim and Tony are going through, it is a good idea to have a number of friends anyway. Expecting one friend to be able to fill all of our needs is an unreal expectation. It sets you up for hurt feelings as people change. The only thing that doesn't change is everyone's desire to be around someone who is kind.

Remember I said at the beginning of the chapter that according to the young people I surveyed, the two top qualities they looked for in a friend were a sense of fun and *kindness*. What may seem "fun" changes as interests change. Being kind to each other is important no matter what changes you are going through. More than anyone else of any age, you can understand what changes your peers are going through. Being kind will not only make you a valued friend and help you "belong" but come back to you when you are in need of a little kindness.

There are two common situations in which kindness is forgotten and the results can be hurt feelings at the least, and a destroyed life at the extreme. These are cliques and rumors—the deadly duo.

Click, Click, Click!

Sandy was part of the best group of friends at school. They all wore their hair pulled back in scrunchies, they sat together at lunch, and they shared secrets. They always tried to wear the same brand designer clothing to the point where others started calling them the "pony club." Sandy and her friends Lissa, Jean, and Barbara didn't mind. It gave them a special identity. They felt they were the "coolest" girls in the seventh grade.

The other girls felt it was an honor to be invited to a party given by one of the pony club members, and to be invited to sit at "their" lunch table was a mark of acceptance. After all, the pony club members were the best, most popular, and most desirable friends to have . . . weren't they? Or were they?

Other girls seemed to ignore the fact that the pony club members spent a lot of time putting down others in their class. In fact, they hurt a lot of feelings by rejecting other girls. They also spent a lot of time making sure that their looks and even their opinions were exactly alike instead of exploring new interests and friendships. A few people just laughed at the pony club members but nobody was laughing when Janie got into trouble for shoplifting.

Janie was a little overweight, wore glasses, and was not considered "cool" enough by the pony club members to sit at their lunch table. She wanted to belong so badly though that since she couldn't afford one of their designer shirts, she tried to shoplift one. Janie got caught and wound up with a juvenile police record.

There are millions of groups like the pony club and they all have one thing in common: they hurt feelings by excluding others. They may not mean to hurt others, but they do and the hurt is real. Any small group that does this is a clique (pronounced click) and they can be very destructive.

As you separate from your parents and develop your own style and identity, it is normal for you to bond with your peers and want to belong to the group. At times you may want to shout out the fact that you are different; and at others, it may feel very important to blend in rather than stand out. That includes wearing a certain style of clothing, liking a certain kind of music, and belonging to a "club." It's great if you are one of the ones who "belong" — it gives a clique a sense of power. But what if you are one of the people who gets rejected?

"I had a couple of friends who started hanging around together all the time," said Karen, eleven. "Then they started being friends with one other girl and if I'd walk up to them, they'd stop talking. Even though they were my friends to begin with, they started excluding me from everything. It really hurt my feelings."

Cliques use their power to hurt and/or to manipulate people. "I had a good friend who became a member of this little clique at school. She started ignoring me," said Bonnie, thirteen. "Sometimes she'd call and say 'If you let me see your English notes, you can sit with the group at lunch tomorrow' or, 'I'll invite you to the party we're having if you loan me some money.' At first I did what she asked because I didn't want to feel left out, but then I decided it wasn't worth it."

Are boys' cliques different from girls' cliques? They seem to be. Boys tend to form cliques based more on a special interest — skate-boarding, for example. If you want to break into the group, you take up the sport or interest. Girls' cliques tend to focus more on manipulating friendships and feelings. In either case, somebody gets rejected and somebody gets hurt.

Coping with Cliques

The three secret weapons are powerful coping tools if you are dealing with cliques. Remember to start with a Reality Check. Ask yourself these questions:

1. What do I want from this friendship? Is it to belong? If yes, what do I have in common with these people?
2. What is the purpose of that group? Are they hurtful to others or are they kind? Do they make people feel good about themselves or generally do they make people feel bad?
3. What are my other options? Are there other people who would make better friends because they are kinder? If I am not accepted by the clique, will it affect my education, my relationships with my family members, and my future? (I don't know of any club that has this power!) What can I spend my energy doing to make myself look or do better?

One middle schooler said that the lunchtime clique at her school got so strong and hurtful that the students asked the administration to get involved. They found a solution in having rotating, assigned seats at the lunch tables so the students would have to sit with new people and get to know others. By doing this for one whole marking period, the clique was broken up and girls discovered new friends they wouldn't have before.

Remember that cliques prevent friendships — not help form them. This is not to say that you shouldn't have a group of friends whom you enjoying hanging out with, but there's a difference between the group who welcomes new faces and the clique that is exclusive and closed. One promotes fun and growth, the other rejects and hurts.

Who Started the Rumor?

"I had a friend who made everybody in school hate me by starting the rumor that I do crazy things," said Nisha, fourteen.

"One of my friends started the rumor that I do drugs, which is not true," said Bill, twelve. "That really hurt."

"I had a friend who told me that guys only liked me for my looks and then I found out she was going around telling everybody that my looks are all I cared about," said Christy, thirteen.

A rumor is a report or statement that is not supported by fact. Sometimes a rumor can be good, as in "People are saying that Jeff is going to win the award for English composition this year." Most often, though, rumors are hurtful. Good rumors are few and far between. Unfortunately, bad rumors are more common and dealing with them is difficult. Rumors are like monsters that rise up and cast a shadow over the person involved. It is very difficult to get out from under that shadow.

Sometimes rumors are started by accident—by repeating someone else's observation as though it were the truth. For example, Rob commented to Phillip that Bart looked sick and he hoped he wasn't doing drugs like his brother. Later in the day, Phillip repeated to Mary that Bart looked like he was on drugs. Within two days, the rumor had spread that Bart was on drugs and that's why he left school at noon. Actually, Bart had a stomach virus but the rumor monster was already growing.

Sometimes rumors are started on purpose. The only reason someone would start a nasty rumor is to hurt, and the person who begins one is an angry person who may need some help from a professional counselor. Often the rumor-starter is jealous of her target, or angry at him, and starting a nasty rumor is her way of "making them pay." Erica was jealous of her friend Pam's looks and popularity. She got very jealous when other girls invited Pam over to their homes and to parties and on shopping trips.

Erica decided she would "fix" Pam. She started the rumor that Pam was gay—that she had seen Pam and one of the female teachers kissing on the lips. Of course, the rumor spread and pretty soon a few parents heard the rumor and called the school. They were concerned about the student and teacher relationship. The nasty rumor was finally traced back to Erica and an ugly confrontation followed. Erica tearfully apologized but the damage had been done. Although both Pam and the teacher were innocent victims, they decided to leave the school at the end of the year because their reputations had been damaged.

Words have power and rumors can grow into powerful monsters. You can stop the rumor monster in one of two ways. First, have no part in feeding the monster. Remember the game of "Telephone" you played when you were younger? That's where you said a simple word or sentence to the person next to you and by the time it had gone through five or ten people, it was completely different. Spreading rumors is like playing the game of telephone. The game is fun, but a rumor hurts a person and generally becomes more awful as it passes from one to another.

Second, if a friend comes to you and says, "Did you hear that Sally ...?" ask some questions. Force a Reality Check on your friend. Ask: Where did you hear that? What proof do you have? What good does it do to talk about someone like this? What are you getting out of passing this information on? Chances are, you will stop the rumor monster right there. Take a Positive Risk and don't be afraid to speak up. Remember, it could just as easily be you that someone is talking about.

If you find that *you* are the one who is the object of the rumor, there is only one effective way of dealing with it. Take a Positive Risk and confront the person who started the rumor.

"My friend and I had a fight and she started the rumor that I was adopted," said Lucy, fourteen. "When I finally traced it back to her, I was really mad. I cried in my room but then I decided to face her with it in front of other people. When I did, she denied it at first. Then she admitted it. We're not friends anymore but if she was telling lies about me, I guess she wasn't much of a friend anyway."

Friends have the Power

What would you say if I told you that you were like a remote control car and you had given the control to someone who could make you move, turn in circles, or just stop whenever they wanted you to? Would you tell me that I'm nuts?

Think about the power you give to your friends. A real friend is someone you can trust with your time, your feelings, your private thoughts. When you entrust your innermost thoughts and feelings to someone, you have given him or her a certain amount of power over you because those you trust can hurt you the most. You don't care as much about those you don't trust. Does this mean that you shouldn't trust or shouldn't care? Not at all! Trusting and caring about others makes life richer and more meaningful. Part of the growth you are experiencing in this stage of your life is learning whom to trust and how to earn the trust of others. Unfortunately, the only way to learn is to make mistakes.

"Bobby and I were really good friends," said Joe, thirteen. "I thought he liked me for me, but I found out that he only liked me because my dad is in advertising and could always get good tickets to games and concerts. I'll never trust Bobby again!"

Pattie found that the person she thought was a good friend also betrayed her trust. "My friend found out that I still suck my thumb even though I'm eleven. She told me not to worry about it because she was sure that lots of people do, but then when we were in front of these guys who were a couple of years older, she told them. I was so embarrassed and so angry at her that I'll never speak to her again!"

Because your friends are important to you, if they say "Boy, you look great today!" you will probably be a little happier and more confident for the entire day, right? By the same token, if a friend tells you, "You're so clumsy, everybody laughs at you!" you'll probably drag around self-consciously all day wondering if everyone you meet laughs at you behind your back.

Sometimes, it is easy to misinterpret friends' actions. Gena was so excited the day she got her first menstrual period that she wanted to share the news with just a couple of her closest friends. She was in the process of telling them, over by the lockers, when

Marsha went up to her locker nearby. The girls stopped talking but stood there grinning at each other. Marsha thought the girls were talking about her and angrily stormed off to her next class to say something nasty about Gena. Imagine Gena's surprise when, after class, two other girls walked up to her and told her off for ridiculing Marsha!

Yes, friends have power . . . but they can also make mistakes. Your self-esteem comes from *you* — not from others. *You* have the greatest power of all over your own emotions and feelings about yourself. By using the three secret weapons when you are faced with friendship conflicts, you will be able to gain some control over the situation.

CHAPTER 7

BUT EVERYONE ELSE LOOKS SO SURE of THEMSELVES

Beth stormed in from school, slammed her books down, and burst into tears. The day had been the pits. Everything that could go wrong, did.

In the cafeteria, she saw her best friend having lunch with Beth's biggest enemy. Beth was scolded by her English teacher for not having her book report done (which she *had* done but forgot at home), and she did not get the part she wanted in the class play. To top it off, she found out that she hadn't been invited to Janet's sleepover party. Beth sobbed because she had no friends, couldn't seem to do anything right, and was the only person she knew who was so miserable. After all, everyone else looked so sure of themselves. What was wrong with her?!

There's no doubt about it, we all have days when everything goes wrong and all we want to do is go home, crawl into bed, and hide. When a little kid has a bad day, he or she can kick a toy, cry, or get into bed and hide! As we get older, however, we discover that we have to continue our day as usual. This gives rise to a very definite personality split when people reach the ages of eleven or twelve — the Public Self and the Private Self.

Your Private Self might dance with a favorite stuffed animal, pick your nose when you're nervous, be afraid to talk to a member of the opposite sex, and still stop to watch Sesame Street with your little brother—and enjoy it!

Your Public Self puts on a cool face and stiff upper lip — unafraid, confident (or at least pretends to be), and "grown-up." Public Selves want to look cool, act cool, and be popular. The Public Self looks at other Public Selves (maybe someone you admire) and says, "OK, *that's* how I'm supposed to act." But inside, your Private Self may be very shy and screaming "Are you crazy? I'll look like a fool if I try this!" At this point, you may be sure of only one thing—that no one else is going through such nervousness, fear, sadness, loneliness, or anger. Stop! Do a Reality Check! With everyone walking around with their Public Self faces on, is it any wonder they look so sure of themselves?

Lee Ann Would Know How to Handle That!

I'll never forget Lee Ann. She was everything I was not. She was tall and blonde, I was short and dark. She could toss her silky hair and it would fall back into place. My hair frizzed and stuck out in all directions. Lee Ann was always beautifully dressed and moved with the grace of a dancer. I always felt as though my slip was showing and everyone could see where I had dropped my chocolate donut on my lap. Lee Ann was an only child and was spoiled with material things. I had two younger sisters and both my parents had to work hard to make ends meet. Lee Ann could talk to boys with a breezy confidence while I choked up at the *thought* of speaking to David, the boy I had a terrible crush on. The only thing that made Lee Ann less than perfect was that she was a little bit of a snob. Instead of being friendly with everyone, she had a way of putting people down which is why I could never understand why she was popular.

I hated Lee Ann. Well, actually, I hated her confidence, her clothes, her popularity, and her attitude. At night, in the privacy of my thoughts, I would devise wonderful ways of humiliating Lee Ann that would make everyone laugh at her, the way she nastily laughed at those who were less confident, beautiful, and popular.

I would compare my Private insecure self to her Public confident one and would look pretty miserable every time. But *that* is what each of us does. No wonder we often come up short in our own minds! I didn't realize back then that you cannot compare a Private Self to a Public Self.

I bet you know a "Lee Ann." Do you compare yourself to her or him and feel less than perfect?

Even famous people who have the admiration of millions occasionally admit to the public that they had terrible anxieties while they were growing up. In a *Glamour* magazine interview, here's what a few of the "beautiful people" agonized through when they were your age. "I had teeth sticking out of my head, cross-eyes, and freckles." — Melissa Gilbert, actress best known for "Little House On The Prairie." Actor and heartthrob Kevin Bacon said "I was a chubby kid." And Morgan Fairchild, a beautiful actress who has appeared in both television and movies said "I never thought I was really pretty because I was so pale—almost white."

Remember how I described this period of your life, in Chapter One, as being like a house under construction? Focus on the part of your house that is already finished. When you are feeling depressed that you: have no friends/are less than great looking/are unsure of yourself/are the only one miserable—Do a Reality Check. Sure, the person next to you may look like he has it all together, but he is probably having a good day and his Public Self is shining.

You are also presenting a Public Self to others, and other people are probably looking at *you* and admiring the part of your "house" that is already in place.

It has been years since I saw Lee Ann. As I have gotten older and a little more experienced, I have realized that she also had a Private Self. Who knows? Maybe her Private Self admired my dark hair, my grades in school, and the fact that I had a larger family than she did. At least, I hope so. It makes me feel better. After all, who knows what goes on in someone else's Private Self?

I'd diE if my fRiENds kNEw tHAt . . .

When you are alone, do you talk to yourself? Imagine that you are a famous rock star? Pick the lint out of your bellybutton and sniff it to see if it smells funny?

Come on, admit it. We all do things in private that may seem babyish or weird — at least that's what our friends would think. Of course, those cool, together people you know probably *never* do anything like . . . well, you know. Right? Guess again!

I asked students in my survey to complete this sentence: "I would die if my friends found out that when I'm by myself, I like to . . ." Here are some of their answers.

"Act like a little kid." —Jay, twelve.

"Sit by the window and cry." —Kate, fourteen.

"Exercise naked." —Jess, thirteen.

"Lip sync songs in front of the mirror or record myself singing so I can hear what I sound like." —Dina, fourteen.

"Take out my old matchbox cars and run them around." —Tom, thirteen.

"Watch cartoons." —Many people said this, ages eleven through sixteen.

"Watch Mister Rogers." —Casey, twelve.

"Kiss my gerbil." —Bobbi, eleven.

"Talk to myself as though there was another person in the room. It helps me sort things out." — A number of kids said this, ages eleven through sixteen.

"Play outside in the rain and pretend I'm a ship captain." —Dick, twelve.

"Read through my little brother's picture books." —Alice, fourteen.

"Sit in the dark and dream." — Several answered this way, ages thirteen through fifteen.

"Talk to my cat/dog/bird." — Many responses, ages eleven through fifteen.

"Sing and dance to songs on the radio, pretending I'm a famous rock singer putting on a concert." —Many responses, ages twelve through sixteen.

"Talk to God out loud at night, pretending He is the Moon." — Allie, fifteen.

Maybe you saw *your* Private Self in these answers. Maybe you could add a new one of your own. Is this crazy, weird, or babyish? NO! It is absolutely normal. It is just what we keep hidden from others because, well . . . it may not look cool.

Be Cool! The Public Self

Matt considered himself a pretty cool guy. He was good looking, a good soccer and baseball player, and had a number of friends to hang out with. But he said he'll never forget his most embarrassing moment. "I was reading out loud in front of the class from a math book and I said 'labs' for 'lbs.' instead of 'pounds.' Everybody started laughing and I turned bright red. That was definitely uncool."

Chevy Chase has made a great career out of doing things in movies that most people consider "uncool." Who else gets paid millions for falling down when most people die inside if they fall in front of others?

"I was trying to be cool, talking to these guys and when I turned to leave, my heel got stuck on a piece of gum and I tripped," said Lisa, fifteen. "Then as I walked away, they kept laughing because the gum had stuck to my shoe and I had these long strings of bubble gum following me."

Horrors! Even worse is when something Private gets exposed to the public.

"I stood up in front of the class to give a book report," said Evan, thirteen. "Everyone kept laughing so I started laughing because I thought they were enjoying my report. When I sat down, my friend said 'You dork! Your fly was open the whole time!' I wanted to hide."

You are probably laughing and glad that what happened to Evan and Lisa didn't happen to you. Or maybe it, or something like it, did and you have sympathy for them. In any case, we all want to look cool and competent. Nobody wants to be thought of as a nerd or a dork. But just what makes a person cool?

I found that being cool had lots of definitions among middle schoolers.

You are cool if you:
- ✔ Do the right thing;
- ✔ Have a girlfriend/boyfriend;
- ✔ Are popular;
- ✔ Are easy to talk to;
- ✔ Dress well;
- ✔ Dress sloppy and are comfortable;
- ✔ Have a good sense of humor;
- ✔ Wear earrings (or an earring for boys);
- ✔ Don't wear an earring (boys);
- ✔ Don't act as though you study hard;
- ✔ Get good grades;
- ✔ Don't get good grades;
- ✔ Don't do drugs;
- ✔ Do drugs;
- ✔ Smoke and don't get caught;
- ✔ Don't smoke.

On the other side of the "cool" coin, there's the friendly nerd (or dork) — the one who makes you cringe if she sits down next to you. But opinions on what makes this person a nerd vary as much as what makes a person cool.

According to middle schoolers, a nerd/dork:

✘ Laughs like a horse;
✘ Laughs at the wrong time;
✘ Thinks they're cool but they're not;
✘ Studies a lot;
✘ Doesn't study enough;
✘ Accepts insults as compliments;
✘ Brags about bad grades;
✘ Brags about good grades;
✘ Smokes;
✘ Does drugs;
✘ Drinks alcohol;
✘ Quotes Pee Wee Herman.

"Actually, being cool or being a dork is really a matter of attitude," said one seventh grader. "You can get straight A's in school and be cool if you don't brag about your grades, or you can be a dork about it and try to make everyone else feel bad."

The cool *Public Self* is a matter of attitude. The person who seems the "coolest" is often the one who isn't pretending to be clever and competent all the time — because nobody is clever and competent all the time! As you use the secret weapons to cope with various situations, you will become more confident naturally. Experience will give you more confidence and that's a "natural cool." But what do you do in the meantime?

COPING — THE NEGATIVE AND THE POSITIVE

Jenny says that when she blows her cool, does something dumb, or has her feelings hurt by a friend, she copes by going on a diet.

Richard says that when he is upset, he either takes it out on his family or sits in the room he shares with his brother and hits the wall.

Beverly says she just cries. Sometimes, she eats anything she can find in the refrigerator, even if she's not hungry.

We all have different ways of dealing with feelings of embarrassment, anger, frustration, and sadness. Some ways can cause more problems than they solve. Others will help turn a crummy situation into the kind of learning experience that will eventually give us the cool confidence we all want.

How do you cope when you are hurt/embarrassed/angry?

When we get into these "uncool" situations, one of the major feelings is that we have lost control in some way — people laugh, a friend hurts feelings, nobody understands. Jenny, Richard, and Beverly were coping by trying to do something that they had control over. Jenny and Beverly could control what did or did not go into their mouths, but that wouldn't help them or the situation and could possibly lead to serious eating disorders. Richard could control how hard he hit the wall, but even though he released tension by hitting the wall, he was hurting his hand — and not helping his situation.

Sixteen-year-old DJ found a different way to cope. "When I got angry or upset — which was a lot — I'd run around the yard outside," he said. "It started by accident and I know I probably looked crazy doing it. The more upset I was, the longer and harder I ran. Pretty soon, I began running down the block and back. Then I ran a few blocks. By the time I got to high school, I was running so much that I made the cross-country and track team my first year!"

Seventeen-year-old Linda also found a better way to cope. "When I was thirteen or fourteen, it seemed as though I couldn't do anything right and I had very little freedom. Everybody else controlled my life. When I was upset over something, I'd clean my room. If that was already clean, I'd clean another room in the house. I remember that one time, I even cleaned my sister's room! She was really surprised. My parents were so happy with me that I got extra privileges. If I had just known, when I was thirteen, that in a few years I'd know how to deal better with things and have more control over my own life, I probably wouldn't have been as miserable as I was."

Nobody likes to have their Private Self exposed and nobody likes to blow their cool Public Self — but it happens to all of us, no matter what our age. Remember the three secret weapons: Do a Reality Check and be a detached reporter. What are the facts of the situation and what is it that you are feeling?

What are your options to Take a Positive Risk? And what can you Coolly Communicate? Sometimes when we blow our cool, we don't think of what to Coolly Communicate until it's too late. (This happens to everyone!) So here are a few lines to help you keep your cool through some embarrassing moments until you think of your own.

Situation: You have fallen down/dropped something/tripped. People are laughing. You laugh and say, "Just think, you pay to see Chevy Chase do this and you got it for free!"

Situation: You discover that your underwear is showing, your zipper is open, or your pants fall down. People are laughing. You laugh and say "That's all folks. The next show is at two o'clock."

Situation: You accidentally burp or fart in public. People are laughing and pointing. You, laughing too, look around on the floor and say "Did anybody see where that frog went?"

Situation: You garble your words when you're trying to sound cool. People laugh. You push your thumb against the roof of your mouth and say "I just have to get these false teeth fixed!"

The main thing is to remember that you *do* live through these experiences and believe it or not, someday they will be funny to you. Keeping your sense of humor — even when it involves *you* — will help you focus on the thought that everyone around you is having moments like that as well. You may just be fooled by their Public Self.

CHAPTER 8

WHEN FUN TURNS INTO TROUBLE!

Most of us, by the time we reach our early teens, know the difference between right and wrong. At least in the most clear cut situations. To kill someone is wrong. So is taking something that does not belong to us. So is attacking someone sexually.

But for many young people, the lines begin to blur when friends get involved in activities that "everybody does." For example, what about cheating on tests (stealing answers)? What about lifting small items from another friend's house or a large store? What about "teaching somebody a lesson" by beating them up after school? Or what about pulling "pranks" like spraypainting a name on someone's house, throwing eggs in their car, or setting a small fire?

And if you have a friend involved in an activity like that, or find yourself caught up in a group activity which turns into something like that, what should and can you do about it?

A time for separating from your parents and thinking for yourself means a time to make ethical decisions that aren't always easy. Unfortunately, a lot of kids are having a lot of difficulty making those decisions correctly. According to an FBI report, forty young people ages ten to twelve were arrested for murder in 1988; 360 for rape; and 1,770 for robbery. Those under the age of eighteen commit 40% of the crimes against property today and account for 28% of the serious and violent crimes overall.

The United States Justice Department released a report that said that the reasons juveniles (usually those under eighteen) give for committing crimes and getting into trouble are: thrill-seeking, attention-getting, adding to their own importance (or status), and the influence of their friends. Rarely does a young person get into trouble all by himself or herself. It usually occurs when friends are together and decide to "have some fun" because they are bored.

"Oh come on," says your friend. "What harm can it do? We're just going to have some fun. Besides, what's the worst that can happen? Nobody's going to arrest us for soaping up somebody's windows!" This is true. You will not be arrested for soaping up somebody's windows, but there is something you should know about the juvenile justice system. You don't have to be arrested to wind up at the police station.

Getting into Trouble

George and his friends were sitting around playing Nintendo one warm Saturday when his buddy had an idea. "Let's go down to the lake," said Tommy. "Sometimes people go away for the summer and you can use their boats and stuff. It'll be fun!"

"But," George objected, "we could get in real trouble. What if the people come back?"

"Nah. What's the worst that can happen? They'll yell at us and we'll say we're sorry but that we didn't think they'd mind if we just borrowed their boat for a little ride while they were away. Anyway, we'll put everything back the way we find it. Don't be such a goody-goody! It'll be fine!"

It was a beautiful day and playing video games *was* getting boring, and as long as they were going to put everything back . . . well, who would get hurt? So George, Tommy, and Frank walked down to the lake. Just as Tommy had said, there were a couple of houses on the lake that looked closed up. The boys wandered around, trying doors. They got lucky at the Smith house — one of the garage doors wasn't locked and neither was the door leading from the garage to the kitchen.

As long as they were there and it was so hot, the boys decided to help themselves to a few sodas. And what's soda without chips, pretzels, and ice cream? Going into the living room on their way out back, they were excited to find a huge entertainment system complete with compact disc player, wide-screen television, and all kinds of tapes. They decided to take the canoe out for a ride first, then come back and enjoy a movie before they went back home.

Playing on the lake was fun — much more fun than playing some dumb video game at Tommy's house. They goofed around, went for a swim, waved at fellow boaters, and then finally dragged the boat back up on the grass. They were just settling down to watch *Die Hard* when the police showed up at the door. One of the neighbors, who knew the Smiths were out of town, saw the boys go into the house after playing on the lake, and called the police.

The three boys were taken to the police station to call their parents. None was "arrested" but they were charged with trespassing and had to go before a juvenile justice committee. Each boy had to pay $50, which he had earned, to the Smiths to compensate for the refreshments they took and to clean their carpet where they had tracked mud from the lake. In addition, each boy had to perform twenty-five hours of community service. They spent a lot of "boring" summer days picking up trash off the road, washing down police cars, and cleaning out the K-9 kennels.

Because you are a juvenile, you are treated differently than an adult who does something wrong or commits a crime. The police and the justice system do try to give you a break on the assumption that you are still learning and will therefore still make more mistakes than an adult. But punishment depends upon the type of wrong you do and which state you live in because the laws of each state are different. If the crime is serious enough, you could also be tried in criminal court as an adult rather than go through the juvenile system.

For example, say you hated your science teacher and wanted to do something to ruin his day. So you and your friend decide to set fire to a corner of the classroom — nothing serious, just enough so you won't have to go to science class for a few days. Well, the fire gets out of hand, reaches the cabinet containing chemicals, which explodes right through the wall into the next classroom where — unknown to you — a student teacher has stayed late doing some work. By the time the fire department puts the fire out, more than $1 million in damages has been done and a person is dead.

It doesn't matter that you didn't mean to hurt anyone. It doesn't matter that you didn't intend to destroy a whole building. If you were fourteen years old and lived in Wisconsin, you would be taken to juvenile court. If you lived in Florida, Colorado, or Connecticut, however, you *could* wind up in adult criminal court. If you committed the same crime and were thirteen years old, but lived in Vermont, Illinois, or Mississippi, you could wind up tried as an adult.

Pretty heavy stuff — but that's just big, serious crimes, you say. *You* don't set fires or do anything really destructive, right? You just play games.

Some "games" are more serious than you might think.

Crank Telephone Calls

Did you ever get a phone call where someone asked, "Is your refrigerator running?"

"Yes," you reply.

"Then you better go catch it!" says the caller, who then hangs up laughing hysterically.

Crank phone calls have probably been made ever since Alexander Graham Bell invented the telephone and they were installed in houses with teenagers. Over the years, crank phone calls have become more threatening, however. In an age when many people live alone and crime rates in certain areas have risen, the crank phone call is rarely laughed at anymore. Even kids who receive them don't think they're funny.

"My friend and I were babysitting my eleven-year-old sister and her friend while my parents were out at a dinner when we got a couple of phone calls," said Russell, fourteen. "The first one just had some breathing, sort of heavy and wheezy. I thought something was wrong with the line so I hung up. A little while later, we got another call. When I answered it, the voice on the other end said 'Six, six, six. Satan is the power. We know where you live and we're coming to get you!' Then he hung up.

"I told my friend and the girls heard it and started to cry. My friend got scared even though he is six feet tall because he had a friend who got mixed up in Satanism and started doing all kinds of horrible things. So I called the police and called my parents who came right home. We never found out who did it, but now I know the right thing to do to trace the call right when they hang up. The police and my parents said it was a crank call, but you have to have a sick idea of what's fun to make a call like that."

Since the innocent "fun" type of crank calls has given way to the obscene or threatening type calls like the one Russell received, many communities now have a tracing system as part of their telephone system. Depending upon where you live in the country, when a crank call is received, you could dial a certain number on your telephone immediately upon hanging up and a trace will be put on the last call you received. The phone company will then call you and say "The trace was successful" or "Unsuccessful." If the trace was successful, a call to the police station will put the gears in motion. By the next day, you and the police will both have a record of who placed the call. Since it will go into the police computer, when complaints come in, they will look at their records to see if the same number comes up again.

"If it's a threatening or obscene call, we go directly to the caller after only one phone call," said a police detective. "If it's kids making the 'refrigerator' type call or just hanging up on the person, we may let it go to three or four. At that point, though, we will call on the parents and discuss what is going on."

Most kids say they make crank calls when there are a few friends together and they're bored. Another "fun" thing to do is to hang around the shopping mall to "pick up" a few things.

Stealing is Stealing

Janie's friend Debra always seemed to have the latest in jewelry and hair clips.

"What size allowance do you get?" asked the twelve year old.

"It's not from my allowance," Debra giggled. "It's from 'the game.'"

"What game?"

Debra lowered her voice so the others in the school cafeteria wouldn't hear her. "I have an uncle who's a security guard in a department store. He said that sometimes they hire people to try to take things to see how good the security is. That's what I'm doing."

Janie's eyes grew wide. "You get paid to steal things?"

"Shh," said Debra. "Not exactly. I just decided to see if there were any security guards at our department store so I took a barrette. It was easy, really. I just stuck it in my hair and walked out. They have so much stuff in that store, I'm sure they didn't miss it. I guess they don't have very good guards because nothing happened. It was so fun!"

"But Debra, that's shoplifting," said Janie. "You could get in trouble."

"Oh come on. If I *did* get caught, I can cry and say it was a mistake — I forgot to put it back. Do you really think they're going to throw me in jail for a barrette?" she said. "Come with me to the mall Saturday. I'll show you how easy it is."

Actually, department store managers and shop owners *are* very likely to come down hard on shoplifters even if the item taken was "just a barrette or pin" and even if the thief is "just a kid." Shoplifting costs the retail industry billions of dollars every year and that's not small change. Shoplifting is a property crime and those under the age of eighteen commit nearly half the property crimes in the country. This is also a very high number and law enforcement officials would like to bring that number down.

If you were to get caught shoplifting, you would still wind up facing the juvenile justice system. You would still be taken down to the police station even if the store, by some small chance, did not press formal charges.

Isn't there a better way to have fun?

What about Mischief Night?

During the late 18th century, some of the immigrant boys to this country brought over the custom of creating a little mischief on Halloween night, like little devils and spirits. They would turn over outhouses, release horses from the pasture, and occasionally break a window.

As Halloween night became more a night for children going from house to house and asking "Trick or Treat," the mischief part of the holiday was forgotten. In some parts of the country, however, the night before Halloween is called Mischief Night and once again, "little devils" go around stirring up trouble.

Some police departments say they are pretty laid-back on mischief night for those who "paper" trees and houses, or soap windows. But window-breaking, mailbox bashing, spraypainting, and car theft will be treated as it is treated at any other time — like the vandalism it is. And vandalism is a crime — not a fun game. Setting off firecrackers and bottle rockets *can* start a fire, depending upon where the sparks land. And shooting a BB gun at someone's house to "scare" them can cause injury and damage that you had not meant to cause.

The point is, all of these actions, which started out being something "fun" and "challenging," can have results which could land you in a lot of serious trouble.

Nobody likes to look like a nerd in front of friends, however. Often, someone will go along with the group—and not participate —but just go along so they don't look like a party pooper. How do you handle this tough situation on your own? Yes, you use the secret weapons.

Taking Control of You

There are a few sayings that have been around for a long time. You may have heard them from parents or teachers. "Birds of a feather flock together," "If you lie down with dogs, you get up with fleas," and "You are judged by the company you keep."

All three of these simply mean that you *will* be judged by the friends you choose to hang around with, because your choice of friends reflects who you are as a person and what you consider important. If those people are troublemakers, some of that trouble will rub off on you.

In more serious terms, if you are with a friend or group of friends who do something wrong or commit a crime, *you* will also be considered guilty simply for being at the scene with them. This is not something you had to worry about as a kid. Your parents tried to select friends for you to play with whom they considered "nice." Besides, what kind of crimes can a six year old commit with parents hovering over them?

Now that you will be on your own more and more, and in charge of making your own decisions regarding friends and activities, *you* are the one who will have to think about this — not your parents.

One of the hardest facts to accept when trying to figure out what to do in situations like this is that most people feel that they can control their friends. "Oh, we will just soap the windows and Vaseline the doorknobs and then we'll stop," you say. "I'm sure that the others won't do any more either. If they want to, I'll just say no and that's it."

One of the *realities* of any situation, though, is that the only person you have control over is YOU. Even with the best intentions, you cannot count on being able to control any of your friends—even good friends you normally trust.

"I work after school, part-time at a vet's office and kennel," said Kara, sixteen. "One of my friends works there, too. I found out recently that she's been taking stamps and other small things from the office like tape, scissors, paper, and folders. I don't know what to do. I don't want to snitch on her, but I don't want to get blamed for stealing. She says that nobody will miss it because offices buy this stuff by the ton. I still think it's wrong and when I told her, she told me I was a dumb jerk. I'm trying to figure out what to do about the situation."

What would *you* do? This is the kind of tough decision that you will have to face at some point. Do you snitch? Do you quit the job even though you haven't done anything wrong? Think about it.

Kara Did a Reality Check and realized that taking those objects is still stealing and they would be missed. Plus, since she could not control her friend's behavior, she was concerned that her friend might progress to stealing money out of the drawer as well. Furthermore, the items were taken during the time that both girls worked in the office. She didn't want to ruin her friendship but she also didn't want to get into trouble and be labeled a thief. That would have a serious effect on her life because she would lose the trust of her parents and others.

Her options were to ignore it and say nothing, tell somebody at the office, quit her job and remove herself, or talk to her friend. Kara decided to talk to her friend first and tell her that she felt taking supplies from the office is wrong and if she didn't stop, she would have to report it to someone so Kara herself wouldn't be blamed.

"It was the hardest thing I've ever had to do," said Kara, her eyes filling with tears. "It ruined our friendship and that hurt. She stopped taking things but I lost a friend."

What Kara did took a lot of guts. Depending upon the situation, you can also use an excuse to help you save face in front of your friends while removing yourself from a bad situation. Going back to the first story about George, Tommy, and Frank, let's see how it could have turned out differently for George if he had handled it in a different way.

Sometimes You Need Help

George could have quickly Done a Reality Check when Tommy first suggested that they go to a lake house and use someone else's boat and equipment. He could have started with his own instincts which were correct: this is wrong and we could get into a lot of trouble.

George had conflicting feelings that he needed to identify. First, he was bored and wanted something fun to do. Second, what had been suggested was wrong. Third, he didn't want to look like a nerd in front of his friends and didn't know how to handle getting out of the situation without looking like a "goody-goody."

George saw only two options: Go along with the group or back out and look like a jerk. He did have another option that he ignored. He could have used his parents as an excuse.

It would be easy for me to say, "Stand up to your friends and tell them that you won't have anything to do with something you think is wrong." Of course, that's the ideal, but few young people would realistically do that. In some cases, it could even be dangerous to sound so goody-goody because of what certain members of the group might do to get back at you.

But it would not have been untruthful to say, "Sorry guys, but my parents would kill me if we got caught. I don't want to get grounded again. I'll have to pass." Or how about if George had looked at his watch and said, "I have to meet my mom to go shopping so I better be getting on." The important thing is he would have taken control over the only person in the situation he could control—and removed himself from a bad scene.

When *you* are faced with a difficult situation involving friends, stop and think before you make a decision. Do a Reality Check: Is the action right or wrong and how do *you* feel about it? If you want attention or acceptance, is the trouble you can possibly get into the type of reputation you want?

Review your options to Take a Positive Risk. If you go along with the crowd just for acceptance, remember that you have handed the control of your actions over to someone else. The only person you can control is you.

If you decide that the activity that has been suggested is wrong, then plan some Cool Communication. You can remove yourself from the situation and still be cool.

The decision whether to get into fun or get into trouble rests in your hands.

CHAPTER 9

Is Just Saying "No" Enough?

Kevin was twelve years old the first time a friend offered him pot at a party. His friend had swiped a joint from his older brother's room and was passing it around. Kevin, remembering all that he had learned in school and from his parents about drug use, said "No." Later that year, at a middle school dance, some friends brought a bottle of vodka to share in the boys' bathroom. Again, Kevin just said "no."

In seventh grade, Kevin was again offered pot at parties and even after school. "What'sa matter, man? You chicken or something?" a few of his friends said. "Look, we do it. Do you see us dropping dead or anything?" Again and again, Kevin said "no."

By the end of seventh grade, Kevin was getting fed up with a lot of things in his life. His parents were always on his case, he was struggling with some difficult classes in school, he missed getting on the school soccer team for the following year, and his friends were still ragging him. At the end-of-the-year picnic, he was offered beer and was about to say no when one of his friends said, "Oh don't bother with Kevin, he's his mommy's little boy. He never does anything wrong." That was it! Kevin took a sip of the beer and passed it on. His friends cheered and the picnic progressed. He had two more quick sips and then made sure he ate plenty of mints before he went home.

As soon as he got home, he ran in and jumped in the shower and brushed his teeth. Even after he was all clean, he was sure his parents would know that he had had some beer. They didn't notice anything.

During eighth grade, having a few sips of alcohol was a pretty regular thing for Kevin. After all, he reasoned, it helped him be accepted, he felt more "grown up" when he drank, and he wasn't hurting anything. He didn't get drunk or sloppy, it gave his whole body a relaxed feeling, and he only did it at parties—never at school. Then at one of the parties, after a few sips of vodka, Kevin was offered a joint. "Sure, why not," he thought, slightly dizzy. "I'll just take one puff and pass it on—just like the beer. No big deal." So that's what he did. He waited to feel stoned but nothing happened.

By the time Kevin was in ninth grade at the local high school, he was facing a lot of different pressures. He was fighting more with his parents, a couple of his teachers got on him about his "attitude," and his girlfriend dumped him for a junior. The only time he felt like he was in control of his life was when he was with his friends, sharing a joint. He didn't have a problem, he told himself, because he controlled when he smoked or drank — it didn't control him. Although his parents knew that Kevin seemed troubled, they never thought he would be involved in drugs—not after all the discussions at school, church, and home! But that was before the accident.

Kevin, fifteen, had gone to a friend's house to hang out and watch videos while his friend's parents were out for the evening. Kevin, his friend, and two others, drank a couple of beers and ate popcorn and chips. Then they shared a joint and ate all the chips and ice cream in the house. That's when they decided to drive to the grocery store and buy some more to replace what they had eaten. One of Kevin's friends was sixteen and was taking Driver Education. "Besides, my dad lets me drive when we get to deserted roads," he boasted. "He says it's good experience." So the boys set off in the family's second car, laughing and joking.

They either never saw the turn in the road, or their reaction times had slowed to the point where the driver — or anyone else in the car — could not turn the wheel fast enough. The police said that the car had crashed into the telephone pole at a speed of fifty miles per hour. Three of the boys were killed. They were fourteen, fifteen, and sixteen years old. One of Kevin's legs was crushed and had to be amputated. He survived but also suffered brain damage and would always have difficulty with his memory. At the hospital, his parents sobbed in each others' arms and cried, "Why couldn't he just say no?"

You have all heard of the "Just Say No!" campaign that was promoted by former First Lady Nancy Reagan. The campaign reminds you to be strong and just say "no" when somebody offers you drugs or alcohol (which is also a very strong drug). Saying "No" is the most important aspect of keeping yourself away from drug and alcohol use, and when you are ten, eleven, or twelve, it's fairly easy to do. As a matter of fact, most kids — just like Kevin — *do* say "NO" the first five or six times that drugs are offered to them.

And then in the middle of adolescence, with everything changing around you, situations which had been clearly "black and white" or "yes and no" before, start to get a little fuzzy. In trying to become an independent person you might think, "Why should I say no to drugs and alcohol just because my parents tell me to? After all, my parents drink. My friends have tried it and say it's no big deal. I'm smarter than those stupid druggies you see on TV commercials — *I* can control myself. If I'm going to be able to keep the respect of my friends, I can just try it once. No big deal, right?"

What's the Big Deal, Anyway?

Did you know that:

- *31%* of all high school students today are drinking in alcoholic patterns?
- More than *one in four* eighth graders said they had five or more drinks on at least one occasion during the past two weeks?
- More than *one out of seven* eighth graders has used marijuana and one out of twenty has tried cocaine?
- There are more known *cancer-causing* elements in marijuana smoke than in cigarette smoke, and that marijuana can do more permanent damage to more of the body's systems than almost any other drug?
- *Six out of ten* emergency room visits related to a suicide or accident involving those aged ten to seventeen were alcohol or drug use related?
- Medical examiners are reporting that of the thousands of drug abuse deaths, those involving youths ages ten to seventeen are rising?

The big deal is that alcohol and other drugs are permanently injuring and *killing* your age group. These statistics were taken from some well-known studies done over the last few years, but even with all those facts, some kids I talked to think that the numbers are made up of "other people."

"Yes, I drink and smoke pot," said fifteen-year-old Penny. "I've done buttons and mushrooms too. I started when I was fourteen. Why not? I do it with my friends. The important thing is not to get too wrapped up in it."

Gloria, fourteen, tried pot with her friend "because we were bored and wanted to see what it was like. I just do it at parties to have a good time." Jack, fourteen, figures that "just alcohol" is OK. "I don't do drugs, just alcohol. I trust my judgment not to do too much."

One of the characteristics of alcohol use, as well as other drugs, is that it does impair your judgment. Even if you are normally a level-headed person, one drink can change all that.

Imagine yourself as the captain of a powerful boat zooming through the waters of a huge lake. Winds blow and try to push you off course, but you use your knowledge to keep your engine roaring and your boat on course. If you see a piece of floating debris, you are able to navigate around it. What a feeling, to be master of this strong vessel, crashing through the waves! Now imagine what would happen if someone came up behind you and pushed a heavy canvas bag down over your head while you were trying to navigate.

Suddenly, you can't really tell what direction your boat is heading. You start to cut back on the power and by slightly turning the wheel, your boat starts going in circles. There's a floating log in the water and you crash into it, which scares you and you jerk the wheel again. Dizzily, you hear a thud and then a crack and you are thrown from the deck. You have hit another boat!

Drinking alcohol or using other drugs is like putting that canvas bag over your head and then trying to be captain of your powerful boat — your body. It cannot be done safely and can result in accidents or even death. Sounds pretty grim, huh? "But," you say, "that's only if you go too far, right? What's the harm in just taking a sip (or a puff) so I don't look like a nerd in front of my friends? Or say I agree with you, how can I say no without looking like a jerk?"

I Don't Want to Look Like a Jerk!

As you separate into your own individual self, you need a welcoming support system of friends. Being accepted is important. What happens, though, when being accepted means doing something that in your heart you feel is wrong or dangerous?

On the one hand, you have your parents, teachers, and other adults telling you that drugs and alcohol can injure or kill you. On the other hand, you have your friends whom you have to face every day, the boy or girl you want to impress, and the feeling that you want to make your own decisions — not just follow along like some three year old. What do you do? It's a tough decision and now that you're beginning to walk away from being a little kid and speed towards being an adult, that decision rests with you.

You may look around and see that some of your friends do drink and experiment with drugs — and nothing has happened to them. Horns didn't grow out of their heads, they still laugh at most of the same things they always laughed at, and their grades in school are OK. Maybe not great, but OK. On top of that, they make *you* feel like a stupid kid by pointing this out and calling you a chicken for not trying something that's "so cool."

When I surveyed or talked to kids about drugs and alcohol, there were three distinct groups. There were those who said "No way, I don't want to put anything in my body that doesn't need to be there!" There were those who said, "Yeah, I've tried it and nothing happened. So big deal! I'll just do it enough to be a part of the group and have fun." Then there were those who said, "I don't think I'd do it, but I'm curious. I'd like to see what happens."

Do any of these sound like how you feel? How do you make an important decision like this? Bring out the secret weapons.

Do a Reality Check!

Doing a Reality Check on a very serious subject like this deserves some serious thinking. You need to both identify your feelings and collect solid facts.

First, your feelings: Do you want to become dependent upon a substance, damage your body for the future, or possibly even wind up dead? Of course not. Your feelings probably center around curiosity or the need to be part of your group of friends. So now we move on to gathering facts.

For help in this area, I consulted several experts in the field, including Dr. Miller Newton, founder of the rehabilitation program KIDS, Inc., the model for the made-for-TV movie "Not My Kid!" Dr. Newton has personally dealt with more than 4,500 kids who have gotten involved in alcohol and drug use. Some of those kids were as young as nine years old. Most of them had been doing well in school to begin with, came from decent families, and said "No" the first few times alcohol or drugs were offered. But they were curious and felt they could "handle it."

Many thousands of kids who thought they could handle it

wound up in the same slide downhill. There are four distinct stages that have been identified as a young person passes from "curious" to "druggie" or "alcoholic."

In Stage One, you've decided to take that drink or joint to satisfy your curiosity or to be a part of the party. The first five or ten or even twenty times you use the stuff with your friends, you find that booze or pot produces a weird change in your body. Your mood goes from "OK" to "mellow or happy." So far, none of the awful things that you had been told would happen, have happened. You don't flunk out of school, go crazy, or get caught. You begin to feel that the adults have lied to you to keep you away from this "wonderful thing." Getting high with your friends becomes a kind of "adult" secret. This stage is called "learning to change your feelings." Your own feelings towards drugs and alcohol start to change from "they're dangerous" to "they make me feel good."

This is when you move on to Stage Two: Seeking the good feeling. Since, so far, you haven't been caught and nothing is going wrong, you start to try to get high whenever you choose. At first it might be weekend parties with friends. Then, it might slip over into weeknights. You blow a big test and then get high to forget feeling bad. Still, you can convince yourself that you're OK because you're not doing it *during* school. But there are other changes slowly going on in your life. You may spend more time alone in your room with the stereo turned up, feeling guilty. You get into more conflicts with your parents and you're afraid they may look at your face and realize you're drinking or doing other drugs and get mad. You may not have messed up your main sport or activity yet, but you give up others because it either "isn't cool" anymore or it cuts into your "relaxation" time.

By Stage Three, as your brain requires more of the drug to get high, you have to spend more money. You may start picking up loose change around the house or dip into your mom's purse. Then you feel guilty over what you're doing and anxious that they'll catch you. You feel bad over the friends you may have dropped, the grades you are blowing, and the activities you've dropped. So you drink or drug yourself more to "fix" those bad feelings. Pretty soon, escaping the bad feelings and getting high becomes the main thing in your life. You are obsessed with getting the good feelings through drugs. At this point, nothing else matters — not school, friends, or family. You may run away from home or get into trouble for stealing to buy your drugs.

When the drug wears off, you feel so ashamed and guilty over what you have done, you struggle to get high again to forget. Your life is now out of control.

You know you are in the Fourth Stage of drug use when you need the drugs in your body just to feel OK enough to get through the day. Your family relationships have fallen apart, you can't handle school anymore, and you begin to have a lot of physical problems because your body is breaking down.

If you don't get professional help by the fourth stage, you die. This is assuming, of course, that you didn't die the first time you tried the drug. Since everyone's body chemistry is different, it is a real possibility that *your* body will have an allergic reaction to the drug and the first time you try it will also be your last.

The reality of drugs and alcohol for adolescents and teenagers is that no drug use is safe at all. Your body chemistry is changing and is quite different from an adult's at this point. Physically and psychologically, your make-up is different. You are still a house under construction and like that house under construction, you can fall apart and blow away in a storm while the finished house can withstand the rain and hurricane force winds.

The final reality of drug use is that it is against the law. Alcohol use is against the law until you are twenty-one. If you use either one, you are committing a crime.

So, where does that leave you? You have done a Reality Check. You have the facts. How do you handle your friends?

Cool Communication

If a friend offers you alcohol or some other drug and you say "No," what will happen? Will they laugh? Call you a baby or a chicken? Leave you out of parties or sleepovers? Pick on you? Is that the *worst* that will happen?

Saying "No" is definitely communicating, but it is no fun to be left out or to be picked on. Fifteen-year-old Tanya found that out. She also discovered something else.

"Last summer I was at a friend's house. There was another girl there and my friend's older brother and his friend. The older brother once used to date my older sister. The brother kept on making fun of my sister and me because neither one of us smoked. He said I was a prude, just like my sister. He had lots of comments and wouldn't stop," said Tanya. "Then he, his friend, and my friend all went outside to smoke a joint. They asked me to go with them and I said no. Then they had more comments for me and I couldn't fight back.

"After a while, my friend came back in the house and asked me if I thought she was a 'bad' person now. At the time I was so embarrassed. They all made me feel so stupid. I just sat in a chair in the corner the whole night and listened to their comments about me being a prude.

"Now that I think back to that night, I'm angry that they did that to me, although I was ashamed and embarrassed at the time. I realize now that I shouldn't feel ashamed of myself because I don't drink or do drugs. Now I'm just angry that they made me feel like I should be ashamed!"

Tanya learned something valuable although that lesson caused her pain. *Just saying "No" isn't enough. You also have to get angry.* How dare a "friend" call you a name for exercising your own free will? Why should *you* feel embarrassed or ashamed because you choose not to go along with the crowd?

If someone says, "What are you, a baby?" you could easily answer, "If I was a baby, I'd follow you. I make my own choices and I *choose* not to." If someone says, "Are you chicken?" you can reply, "Of course! Only a fool would not be afraid to put chemicals that could kill you into their body. Would *you* drink gasoline?"

You don't need to be defensive — *they* do. Getting angry that someone would call you names or pick on you for not trying drugs or alcohol brings you to the third secret weapon.

Take a Positive Risk

What is easier — to go along with the group and be accepted or to stand alone? Which takes more strength? Which person is looked up to more — the person who says "yes" to blend in or the person who has the courage to disagree with the group?

Undoubtedly, it takes more strength to say "No" and stand apart from the group. It also does something else. It gives you power.

Think about your options. You can join in and hurt yourself, but not make waves with your friends, or you can resist and show that you think for yourself. Do you know what they call people who think for themselves? Leaders. And you will not be alone. In spite of the numbers of kids who are involved in drugs, those of you who say "no" are still in the majority. You have to be as aggressive at getting *your* point across as the druggies are. One middle-schooler took a risk and found this out.

Kate, an eighth grader, was hurrying to her next class when a well-known school druggie brushed up close by her. "Here honey, this is for you," he said, and shoved a vial of crack into her hand. He hurried on down the hall, grinning, and Kate was left wondering what to do. But only for a minute.

Hurrying into her next class, she handed the vial to the teacher and reported what had happened. "I'm not involved in this," she said. "It's wrong and I don't want to get caught." She gave the teacher the pusher's name and told her that he probably had more.

The school principal had the druggie taken into custody and checked his locker. Sure enough, there was enough crack in the locker to wipe out the whole school. The police were called in and the druggie was taken to face juvenile court. Although some of his friends made threats against Kate, the rest of the kids who were sick and tired of drugs being passed in their classrooms and halls came forward to protect and praise her.

The druggies in that school have now been put on notice that they *are* a minority and an unwelcome one. All because the rest of the kids not only said "no," but they got angry as well!

If you Do a Reality Check, Communicate, and then Take a Positive Risk by choosing to withstand the pressure of joining in, you will probably be surprised to find that there are many who feel the way you do. Sometimes, even those who pressured you in the first place come to respect you for having the courage to think for yourself. A former professional athlete I know, who still does not drink alcohol, said that you just have to be firm in your belief and stick to it. "Everyone knows the stuff is no good for you, so only idiots are going to tease you about not taking a drink," he says. "Are you going to listen to idiots?"

Remember, you don't have to please anyone but yourself. The decision you face whether to do drugs and alcohol or not is not your parents' decision, teachers' decision, or friends' decision. It is *your* decision, and one that will affect the rest of your life.

PART THREE

YOU AND SCHOOL

CHAPTER 10

My Whole Life is Graded!

Glenda is expected to bring home straight "A's" in school. When the sixth grader got a "B" on her report card, her parents grounded her for a month and took away her Nintendo until the next marking period.

When Janice gets a bad grade on a paper or test, she cries. She has begged teachers to let her redo the work so her parents wouldn't find out. She then punishes herself by not eating and uses that meal time for her studies.

Aaron is expected to go into the family business someday. Although he is only in eighth grade, his grandparents are already pressuring him to excel in math and the sciences so he can join their medical practice. Aaron dutifully struggles with the sciences but is a gifted writer — a talent his grandparents call "a playtime activity."

Life is full of competition, no matter what your age, job, or social circle. When you were in nursery school, you may have tried to run faster than Billy, build blocks higher than Susie, and throw a spitball farther than Jeff. That spirit of competition may have been softened in elementary school by some adults saying, "It's more important that you learn than get a good grade" or "It's more important that everyone gets to play during the game, rather than just use the best players."

Now, all of that is changing. Parents who see college or jobs down the road for you may be applying pressure on you to excel. For many like Glenda, Janice, and Aaron, it's no longer "It's more important that you learn something," but rather, "What do you mean you got the third highest grade in the class? Why didn't you beat out the other two?" All of a sudden, it seems everything you do is being graded at school, on the playing field, and even at home.

At this point, some students start to wonder, "Will they love me only if I get good grades?" Or as one seventh grader said, "When I get a bad grade, I get upset because I feel as though I'm failing my parents."

Parents aren't the only ones applying pressure. Students do it to themselves and then fall apart when they get a bad grade. After all, an "A" means you are a success and an "F" means you are a failure, right? Wrong. Neither is completely true and neither is fixed in stone.

It is important to mention right up front that I had to Do a Reality Check in preparing this chapter because I found that many of you have different ideas as to what constitutes a "bad" grade. When asked, 50% of the students said that a "C" would be considered a "bad" grade, although "C's" are described as representing "average." Tying for second place in the bad grade category were a "B" and a "D," with 20% of you voting for each. While getting a "D" was definitely bad, differences in the kind of "B" that constituted a bad grade were made by many. For example, a "B+" was considered OK, but a "B-" was considered "bad" by some. Finally, 10% answered that an "F" was a bad grade and one sixth grader made the additional comment that for him, a "C" would be a good grade!

As you can see by this small sampling, there are many different opinions as to what makes a "good" and "bad" grade. Just as there are many opinions and needs that take the form of pressure on you.

Who's Holding the Yardstick?

The scene was Back To School Night for parents to meet the teachers and administrators and ask questions they might have concerning their children's programs and progress. During the course of the evening, one father approached his son's teacher and asked, "From what you've seen so far, do you think my son is Harvard material?" Before the teacher could answer, another father jumped into the conversation and said, "Harvard? Kathy's going to Princeton. Why would you mess around with Harvard?"

A mother who had been standing nearby joined the conversation. "Don't forget Berkeley. *That's* a great school. Besides, you can always go Ivy League for graduate school." The teacher, who had not been given the chance to really answer the first question, just stared at the parents in horror. These were not parents of high school students ... or even middle school students. Hers was a third grade classroom! You've probably met some parents like that. Or one like Mr. Jones who, when he found out his eleven-year-old son Vic liked basketball, decided that Vic was going to be a BASKETBALL STAR. Dad drilled Vic on hook shots and fade away jumpers and had him dribbling before breakfast and after dinner. Weekends were no longer spent with friends or going to the movies but rather driving to watch basketball games — high school, college, and pro.

Mr. Jones brought home posters of basketball stars and pinned them up around Vic's room — right next to the nutrition chart he ordered from the NBA. Finally, one day, Mr. Jones was shocked when he came home to find Vic tearfully stabbing the basketball with his Swiss army knife. The reason? During tryouts that day, Vic had frozen under the pressure. He didn't make the school junior varsity team.

Did Mr. Jones hate Vic? Is that why he drilled him, drove him, and coached him? No. In fact, Mr. Jones loved his son very much. So did Janice's parents, Glenda's parents, Aaron's grandparents, and the third grade parents who were discussing their college choices. Most parents want only the best for the children whom they love, whether that's clothes, lessons, schools, jobs, or sports careers. But sometimes, parents who are enthusiastically pushing for the best for their child mistakenly push *the child* too early, too strongly, or just too much and forget that lots of mistakes get made along the way to success.

By the same token, most kids want to please their parents, so they at least try to be the best, do the best, and go for the best. The problem is, since we all make mistakes, it is impossible to *always* be and do the best. That's life.

When being the best becomes the most important thing in your life, to the point where you feel that making a mistake means your life is over, something is very wrong. You have let the competition rule *you* instead of *you* taking charge and ruling yourself. That includes learning how to cope in a positive way when you blow it.

This is not to say that you shouldn't always try your best. On the contrary. In fact, that's one of the aspects of Taking a Positive Risk — you are trying your best; you are trying something new.

Sometimes it works, sometimes it doesn't, but the experience helps you to grow and be that much more capable the next time around. Mistakes are going to be made along the way but remember, you're still that house under construction. There's plenty of time to change a wall around, move the staircase, or add a window! That is something that Benny's father didn't seem to realize.

"I know my dad has his heart set on me going to Princeton, someday," said the eighth grader, "but my grades are terrible. I know I've failed him, but B's and C's are what I seem to get even though I try. There are five kids in my family and we live in an apartment that's a little crowded. Dad wants us to make something of ourselves so we can be successful and have a big house if we want it.

"My older sister was almost a straight 'A' student and he expects the same of me. When he sees a 'C' on my report card, sometimes he doesn't talk to me for days."

It would be easy to get huffy and say "Well, Benny's *dad* is the one with the problem, not Benny!" and of course, in one sense, you would be right. Benny's dad wants a better life for his children but he's only looking at one way to reach that goal. When his son doesn't "measure up," he gets afraid for him and then angry.

But it is Benny's problem as well because *he* has to live with his dad. When his dad didn't talk to him, Benny would get so mad inside that he would go out and break things. At first, it was little things like breaking toy cars and glass jars and ripping books. Lately he's been taking his anger out on bigger things. He attacked a parking meter with a skateboard, breaking both. If Benny doesn't find another way to cope, he will wind up in big trouble.

How do *you* cope when you get a bad grade or when you feel you don't measure up? A lot of people cry. Some said they yell at someone else or go off by themselves to be upset. A few said that they ask the teacher for a meeting to discuss the bad grade. I recommend using the Secret Weapons.

Making the Grade — Your Way!

First answer this question and be honest: Is it realistic to assume that you are going to do everything right, all the time?

Of course not. Then is it realistic to *expect* yourself to *always* do the right thing and get the perfect grade? Of course not. So starting from *that* point, Do a Reality Check. What is it that you want and what is it that you feel?

It *is* realistic to want to please your parents, perform well, and be admired. It is *not* realistic to think there is only one way to meet those needs. Part of Doing a Reality Check is finding balance.

Emily blew her science quiz and missed the basket that would have won her team the game. But in the same day, she helped a fifth grader with a math problem at lunch. Were the bad grade and missed basket going to ruin her life? "It was just one bad grade," said Emily. "There are always going to be more tests. That was just one of many. Of course I felt bad, but you just have to go on."

It is easy to look at a mistake you have made or a test you have blown and think that you are defined by that one mistake. It is easy, but it isn't true or realistic.

Imagine your life as one long road with twists and turns, wide spaces and narrow spaces. In some places you can see ahead and in some, you can't. Now as you are walking down that road, if you trip over a pebble or step in a pothole, you just recover your balance and keep on walking. You don't stop and say you can't finish. Those mistakes and bad grades are the pebbles and potholes. They are not pleasant, and you may lose your balance for a moment but you keep on going to the smoother road ahead because the road continues; it does not end just because there's a pebble in the way.

It is human nature to focus on what is wrong — the problem instead of the smooth road. When you hit a rough spot, however, you need to remind yourself that there are also things that you do right. The day that Emily blew both her test and her basketball game, she could at least feel good that she helped a fifth grader out. When you blow it, look for something positive about yourself. If you have to, sit down and make a list. What are you good at? Listening to a friend? Art? Throwing a ball? Some days, it may only be that you said hello to the dog or cat and they were happy to see you. But that's balance, and that's realistic.

Setting Goals Helps

Goal setting is important to finding a balance in dealing with school pressure. In Taking a Positive Risk, you set specific and realistic goals.

Jerry used to say, "I want to do well in school." He kind of muddled along, hoping all would be well. Then, if he didn't get the marks he thought he deserved, he would sulk and be upset. Often he would blame the teacher. Jerry needed to make his goals more specific, however.

"Doing well in school" is very general. It could mean anything from "being popular" to "getting straight 'A's.'" That is very hard to focus on and figure out a plan of attack. When things go wrong, you can feel out of control. A more specific goal would be "I would like to get an 'A' on my social studies test this week." Chances are, you can figure out how to work towards that. The teacher has probably told you what to study. You can make sure you set aside extra time to go over the material. Then, you do your best. If you do well, congratulations! If you fall short of your expected grade, you will have a specific plan of attack for next time.

"When I get a bad grade, I just try to forget it as soon as possible," said Chris, an eighth grader. "Sometimes it was an unfair test or grade, sometimes I just blew it for stupid reasons. But when you look at your whole life, one test or grade isn't going to kill you or make you a bad person. You just go on and try to do better next time."

OK, so you have looked at the situation realistically. You have set specific goals for yourself. You have made a list of the good things you do and the talents you have. How do you communicate that to the people who are saying, "What do you mean you only got a 37 on your math test?!"

But I Don't Want to Be A Doctor; I Want to Play with Puppets!

I remember reading an interview with Jim Henson, the creator of the Muppets. He grew up in a pretty traditional house with hardworking parents who wanted him to do well and succeed. But their idea of success for their son Jimmy was more along traditional lines. Henson said in the interview that his father was convinced that his son wouldn't amount to much because he wouldn't get serious about anything but playing with puppets. Of course, Jim Henson was wonderfully successful and you are probably familiar with his many Muppet characters through "Sesame Street," the movies, television cartoons and specials, and all the Muppet products and books. That's one father who was probably delighted that he was wrong.

Jim Henson's father loved him and wanted only what he thought was best for his son. Your parents love you and want you to be the very best you can be. Sometimes their enthusiasm towards that end might make you feel that you are only good if you are getting good grades. By the same token, you may feel that you are bad or unlovable when you get bad grades or goof up in some way. Neither of those is true and you should give your parents the opportunity to let you know it.

Sure, there are going to be times when you are both disappointed that you did not "perform" as well as you both expected. That's life. You can let them know how you feel by saying, "I really tried, but I guess I blew it. Next time, I will (fill in the blank with something specific) to do better." Then ask your parent if he or she remembers a time when *they* blew something important and ask, "How did you deal with it?"

This accomplishes two things. It lets your parents know that you are trying. It also forces them to remember what it's like to mess up and feel bad. We all need gentle reminders from time to time.

In communicating your feelings to your parents, you also need to Do a Reality Check as to whether their expectations for you are unreasonable. If they are simply encouraging you to do your best — that is reasonable. It is part of their job as parents to guide you to find the best in yourself and use your talents and abilities.

If, however, you feel so unreasonably pushed that you have considered running away from home, suicide, or other violence rather than bring home a bad grade or bad news, you need some serious help. If communicating those feelings directly to your parents hasn't worked, try to find another adult whom you trust or an older sibling to talk with them on your behalf. The important thing is to communicate!

Setting realistic goals, offsetting a negative with a positive, and viewing your life as a long journey will help you take control and find the balance you need when you feel your whole life is graded.

CHAPTER **11**

GIVE A REPORT?
Gulp!

Cindy thought she was going to die.

The weight on her chest was so heavy that she couldn't breathe. Her body began to jerk out of her control. Sweat was trickling down the small of her back and behind her knees. She tried to move her mouth but her tongue had swollen up and stuck to the roof of it. She looked out and saw fifty hardened eyes staring at her. The small bumps on her face began to throb and her mind saw them exploding, one after another like Fourth of July firecrackers. Cindy's last thought before she wet her pants was "I know Mrs. Freeborn is going to give me an 'F' on this!"

Cindy wasn't being tortured. Well, not really. She was standing up in front of her third period history class where she was supposed to give an oral report on Patrick Henry. She looked at his famous cry "Give me liberty or give me death!" and thought she would prefer death to giving oral reports!

While most kids would not prefer death, most said they would rather have a tooth pulled at the dentist rather than have to stand up in front of a classroom of their peers, or an audience of friends and relatives to give a report or play performance. They are not alone! Famous actors confess that they feel sick to their stomachs before they go "on." Professional television newscasters like Barbara Walters and Charles Osgood have written articles and books which share stories about the times they have goofed up in public, giving advice to adults who have to do the dreaded task — speak before groups.

Giving reports and performing before others are part of life, however. In fact, the more successful you are, the more you are called upon to do it. That doesn't mean that the nervousness goes away — you just learn to cope with it better. A Reality Check will show you that even if you *do* flub up, the world doesn't end. (Although you might wish the ground would swallow you!)

You — The Speaker

The four main reasons beginning speakers would rather face a dentist than an audience are:

What Will I Say To Make Them Listen?
I'm Too Shy!
Everyone Will Think I'm A Fool!
I Always Feel Uncomfortable In Front Of People.

Let's look at these one at a time.

What Will I Say To Make Them Listen?

The most obvious answer is, Do Your Homework! That is, if you have to give a book report, spend some time on it. Try to make it interesting. If it was a dull book in your opinion, make your comments on it creative — such as how it could have been improved. If you are doing a play, study your lines so you have something to say. If you are doing a report for social studies, science, or any other subject, try to find a little-known or interesting fact about your topic. This way, you will be eager to share something that no one else knows — maybe not even your teacher.

Then practice your report out loud a couple of times. This really helps. When I have to give a speech, I practice out loud as I walk around the house, drive in the car, or just stare out a window. If you are familiar with your report, by the time you give it, you will have a little more confidence that even if you goof up, you'll be able to find your place again!

I'm Too Shy!

Stanford University did a survey which showed that 40% of the *adults* they polled described themselves as shy. If you asked around your school and neighborhood, you'd probably find that 90% of your friends describe themselves as shy and the other 10% are putting on their Public Self.

Being shy is just another way to describe being unsure in new or special situations, and your life is probably full of those right now. But if you Do a Reality Check, you may discover that you aren't *always* shy. After all, you are not too shy to go to the movies, are you? Of course not. You have gone to the movies since you were a little kid. You know how to go up to the box office, tell the ticket person which movie you want to see, pay for the ticket, and make your way into the correct theater.

Now if you were a visitor from Mars and you were trying to see what a movie theater was all about, you might be a little shy. The whole process of going to the movies would be unfamiliar to you. Speaking in public, acting in a play, and giving a report are still unfamiliar situations to you. The more practice you have doing them, the less frightening they will become. You may still be nervous — but you won't be scared to death!

Everyone Will Think I'm A Fool!

"When I was twelve, I had to get up in front of my church to read a part from the Bible for a Christmas play," said Jon, thirteen. "There was a wire running from the podium to behind the scenes. I didn't see the wire and tripped and fell into the wall that was supposed to be the background for the manger. All the walls started falling and the whole church was laughing. I was so embarrassed!"

Too bad a videotape wasn't going or Jon could have sent it to "America's Funniest Home Videos" and turned an embarrassing moment into cash. He may have been embarrassed, but he lived through it and can now sympathize with others who are struggling to perform.

Think of the last time you had to stand up before a group and give a report or speech. What was going through your mind? I used to be sure that everyone could see that I had one arm longer than the other, that my skirt was wrinkled, that I was too fat, that I had a big zit that glowed in the dark forming on my chin, that my hair was too frizzy, and that my breasts weren't very developed.

Do you know what they were *actually* thinking? "Oh my gosh, the teacher's going to call on me next!"

That's right. Your audience may be looking at you, but the only relaxed people in the room are the teacher and the kids who have already given their reports. The rest are worrying about what *they* are going to say, how *they* look and hoping that *they* don't fall down, throw up, or wet their pants! Now doesn't that take the pressure off?

What happens if you *do* trip, forget your lines, or realize you've garbled your words? You go on . . . continue. Laugh too, if you can and keep on going. You may feel dumb because you did something less than perfect but you won't look like a fool—you'll look just like the rest of us—human. There isn't one person alive who has given an oral report or play performance and hasn't messed up. Not one! Even President Gerald Ford tripped a couple of times when going to give a speech, and President Ronald Reagan mixed up his words! When the President of the United States goofs, the whole world sees it. When you goof, only a handful of kids in a classroom see it. So take a deep breath and try again!

I Feel Uncomfortable In Front Of People!

Here are some tips from other middle schoolers who try to face giving a report calmly.

"I always wear comfortable clothes that I like," said Phil, fourteen. "I used to think I had to wear something new, but once when I wore a new shirt, the tag in the back kept irritating me and that's all I could think about. Now I wear comfortable stuff."

"I practice in the mirror first so I'll know how my face will look when I'm saying different things," said Lauren, twelve.

"I use props," said Martin, thirteen. "I never know what to do with my hands and that makes me nervous so I either carry a pencil and fiddle with it, or maybe a quarter in my pocket. Just something for my hands to hold."

"Once during a history report I was giving, some people walked out of class. That really upset me," said Doris, fourteen. "So now I try to speak a little louder than I usually would and even change my voice. Maybe that way, people will stay awake or think they'll miss something interesting if they leave."

Finally, on a very practical note — remember to keep breathing and go to the bathroom before the class where you have to give a report.

It may sound funny to tell you to keep breathing but when we get tense, we tend to hold our breath. That only adds to nervousness. Athletes before a game or match will spend some time breathing deeply. This floods the body with oxygen, calms nerves, and prepares the body for deliberate action. Giving a report can feel like an athletic test, so think about breathing. You may find yourself speaking more slowly and calmly.

Also, go to the bathroom before your report. There's nothing worse than that feeling like when you're playing Hide and Seek, and you're hiding and the person who's It is getting close, and you get nervous and feel like you have to go to the bathroom. In the game, you only have to yell "Boo!" When you give a report, there's a whole lot more to say and you don't want to be worried that you may not make it!

The Audience Wears Underwear!

Even if you have prepared your report, are wearing your favorite clothes, and have visited the bathroom, you still have to face an audience of listeners. Even listeners who are all worried about their own reports have eyes that stare up at you. This is the toughest part of the whole deal—facing those eyes.

Experts who advise those people who must routinely get up before crowds, such as business leaders, politicians, educators, and news people, offer a little trick. Act "as if" you were confident. Act "as if" facing the crowd is no big deal. In other words—ACT!

Maybe you, Bobby Jones, are nervous over presenting a book report, but Bobby Jones, TV anchorman, could read that report without blinking. Act "as if" you were Bobby Jones, newscaster. Sometimes taking on the role of someone more confident helps us get through those times when our own confidence needs a boost.

But each of us has a different way of coping. These are some suggestions that have worked for sixth, seventh, and eighth graders.

"I find one person I can look at — usually a friend — and only talk to that one person in the audience."

"I look at the back of the room so I don't have to look at anyone's eyes. Other people's eyes make me forget what I'm saying."

"I pretend there's no one in the room and that I'm alone."

"I pretend that I'm on a TV game show."

"I try not to be so serious. I like to put a joke in my reports. Even if it doesn't really fit in, everyone laughs and I relax."

And one seventh grader suggested: "Imagine that everyone in the room is sitting there with their underwear on their heads! But you have to be careful," he said, "because you can get laughing so hard that you won't be able to give your report. I know!"

If *that* doesn't help relax you, I don't know what will.

CHAPTER 12

SURVIVING AN UNFAIR TEACHER

Tony's science teacher is also a coach. If someone is good on the athletic field, he will tend to mark them up in science. If not, they pay a price.

Beth's English teacher shows extreme favoritism towards the boys in the class. She has also targeted Beth as her least favorite student. While the boys get away with being lazy, the girls don't get away with anything, and Beth is constantly struggling just to stay even.

Kurt's math teacher yelled at him for turning in a sloppy looking paper and demanded that he redo it. Kurt spent nearly two hours carefully reworking and copying problems. When he presented it to his teacher the next day, however, she took it and without looking at it, dropped it in the garbage can in front of Kurt.

One of the realities you may be facing is that not all teachers are created equal. Some are incredibly dedicated, sensitive, creative, and caring. Most are competent and genuinely interested in sparking a love for learning in their students. Then there are those who do not have the patience and energy to teach, don't really like kids, or take their personal problems out on students in the classroom. Although these teachers are in the minority, everyone seems to get at least one during their school career.

If a kid's job is going to school, then the teacher can be compared to a boss. Both a boss and a teacher have the power to affect their workers. A boss has power over an employee's money. A teacher has power over a student's grades — which can also affect a student's homelife.

It is a very frustrating feeling to have so little control over a very big aspect of your life. This is particularly true as your sense of what is fair or unfair becomes sharpened. If you find yourself in the classroom of a teacher you think is unfair, be aware that you are not alone. Three out of four of those students in my survey said they had had unfair teachers. The four top complaints were: Favoritism (several different forms); Teachers Who Humiliate Students; Incompetent or Lazy Teachers; and Teachers with Unfair Work Habits.

Are you totally powerless when faced with a teacher who picks on you, gives you a week's worth of work in one night, calls you names in front of others, or gets angry if you ask a question? Not completely, but this is a difficult situation as you probably already know, and it calls for not only the Secret Weapons, but possibly help from other sources.

Before we discuss tactics, however, let's take a look at what makes a teacher unfair.

TEACHER'S PET, TEACHER'S POISON

Sally and Jess are both in eighth grade at the neighborhood middle school. Sally's mother, Mrs. Jakes, is both the English teacher and the eighth grade coordinator, which means she's in charge of most of the class activities. Because Mrs. Jakes wields a certain amount of power both in and out of the classroom, Sally enjoys a big advantage. If a person is Sally's friend, Mrs. Jakes favors them with privileges. If Sally doesn't like someone, neither does Mrs. Jakes and privileges, positions, awards, and activities are withheld accordingly. In the classroom, Mrs. Jakes rarely gives anyone a higher grade than Sally. Since most of the work is essay, this is difficult to argue against because the grading is subjective. And around the school, Sally gets away with actions that would — and do — land other kids in detention. She plays tricks on kids, uses foul language, and deals her friendship out as though it was a queen's jewel. Some kids "suck up" to Sally to get in good with Mrs. Jakes, although they confess that they really don't like her. Others just stand back and hope not to cause Sally — and thereby Mrs. Jakes — to be angry with them. In either case, most of the classmates say they can't wait for the year to be over so they won't have to pretend friendship to protect their grades anymore.

Teacher's "pets" have been around as long as there have been teachers and students. It is natural for a teacher to have a special liking for one or more students, just as you have a special liking for one or more adults with whom you come in contact. What makes the "teacher's pet" situation intolerable, though, is when the teacher can't keep his or her feelings under control and allows that favorite excessive privileges or grades that are unavailable to the rest of the students.

It is not that often that a teacher has his or her own child in their classroom. When it does happen, in many cases the parent tends to be harder on their own child. In some, like Mrs. Jakes and Sally, the favoritism gets out of control.

"We had to give a presentation on Russia," said Donna, fourteen. "I spent more than five hours on mine and thought it deserved an 'A.' My friend, who is our social studies teacher's favorite, threw hers together before school and during lunch. She got an 'A-' and I got a 'C+.' I don't think either of those grades was fair."

Mark, a seventh grader, also has a problem with a teacher showing favoritism. "There's a girl in my science class who can almost turn in a blank piece of paper and get an 'A.' This practically happened one time when we had a big homework assignment. She didn't do it. When we handed in our papers, the teacher asked her where hers was and she said she forgot because she had gone to a concert the night before. He said, 'Well, you know this stuff anyway, just write it out real quick now. You don't have to give me details.' So she did. Other times, if anyone else doesn't hand in their work, we get extra work on top of the original work and no excuses are accepted. Not even going to concerts!"

Sometimes teachers show favoritism towards boys or girls as a group. This, of course, does nothing to further good communication between the two sexes.

"Our math teacher favors the girls. She even told us that and then laughed, but it's true!" said Jim, thirteen.

"My Spanish teacher likes the boys and only puts up with the girls," said Stephanie, fourteen. "She gives them more time to answer and never criticizes their papers for being sloppy like she does the girls'."

"On the first day of school, my science teacher said 'OK men, let's show the girls which is the smarter sex.' He definitely favors the boys in the class," said Monica, twelve.

Then there's the teacher who picks a favorite based on a special interest, like Tony's science teacher who passed out science grades depending upon how well the student did on his team.

It's a funny thing about the teacher's pet, though. Being the teacher's favorite often lands him or her in the position of being the least favorite (sometimes "most disliked") among the students. This is the opposite of the student who is sometimes dubbed the "teacher's poison" — the one who gets picked on the most.

"I hate it when the teacher picks on one student all year long, even though that kid hasn't done anything special to deserve being picked on," said Nelly, twelve.

Danny, thirteen, agrees. "There's this one kid in my social studies class that the teacher yells at for every little thing — like even if his feet aren't flat on the floor. But I've heard that he does that every year — picks on one person all year as an example. I don't think that's fair."

Favoritism is difficult to fight because first of all, the person receiving the "favors" isn't about to complain. Second, unless the teacher's actions actually hurt you in a tangible way, you have very little ammunition. All you can do is what is expected of you, following directions to the letter.

If you feel you are the "poison" or the picked-on "example" for the year, you can follow the steps we'll discuss at the end of the chapter to try to change the situation.

FACE IT — YOU HAVE NO TALENT!

There are very few students today who didn't sit in front of the television set and watch as Mister Rogers changed into his sneakers and sweater. During the half hour of being in his "neighborhood," Mister Rogers would constantly tell you how wonderful and amazing you and your body are. And didn't it make you feel warm when he'd end the show by saying "I like you just the way you are!"?

Unfortunately, you then go to school and expect all of your teachers to be as warm and sensitive to your feelings as Mister Rogers was. Many are, but there are some who need to be reminded that students *have* feelings.

"I really enjoyed art and worked hard on my projects," said Kara, fourteen. "Then I got this one art teacher who just thought he was so tough and that teaching us kids was really beneath him. I had worked real hard on this collage. I spent hours collecting things to put together. When I turned it in, he just looked at it and laughed and said in front of all the other kids in the class, 'Face it kid, you just don't have any talent.' I was really crushed. It made me cry. I've never liked art class since and that happened when I was twelve."

Being put down in public is embarrassing, no matter what your age. Although some students commented, "That's how some teachers get their kicks," others said, "Don't they care?"

"I was assigned a paper and couldn't find much information on the subject. When I told the teacher, she said she understood," said Dina, fifteen. "Then I turned it in. I was in another class and she came storming into the classroom and screamed at me in front of the whole class that I didn't type the paper — which I didn't know I had to — and that if I didn't get more information, redo the paper, and type it, that I would fail the course. It was so embarrassing! Couldn't she have called me into the hall or told me that in private?"

"I know teachers are human," said Tracey, fourteen, "but so are kids. I can't stand having a teacher yell at me that I'm dumb just because I made a mistake. I've had a couple of teachers like that and I wind up being afraid to do anything in their class because it will be wrong." The teacher who screams and belittles students has forgotten how to interact. Almost as tough to deal with is the teacher who doesn't *want* to interact.

Don't Question Me!

If you ask any ten of your friends, "What's a teacher supposed to do?" they will probably answer, "Teach" and look at you as if you had just landed from Mars. But if you pushed it a little further and said, "How does a person teach?" you might get a couple of different answers. "By helping you learn new information." "By answering questions." "By showing you how to find answers."

Those *are* all things a teacher is *supposed* to do, but some students are trying to struggle along with a teacher who won't or can't answer questions and help them learn new material — because they don't know it themselves! And if you ask a question, they get angry because it makes them look dumb.

"I was stuck with a science teacher who just stayed one step ahead of us in the book," said Ginny, fifteen. "Most of the time, if we asked questions, he didn't know the answers. His classes were so boring because all he did was say, 'read the book.' There was one kid in class who was a real science nut and he was always making things and reading up on inventions and discoveries. Whenever he asked the teacher a question, the teacher would get angry and tell him he had a bad attitude. It was the worst year!"

"I have a social studies teacher who is so lazy!" said Dina, fourteen. "She assigns reading in the textbook to us and then sits at the back of the room reading romance novels. If you ask her a question, she just says 'Look it up.' Sometimes she doesn't even make out her own tests. The pages look like they come from some manual and sometimes they have questions on stuff we haven't even covered. That's not fair!"

"It's really unfair when a teacher won't answer questions," said Tommy, twelve. "When I don't understand something, and go to ask a question, she won't answer. She just says, 'You should have known that.'"

Then, of course, we have the opposite of the teacher who doesn't want to be involved in your work—the one who goes over-board in assignments, projects, and tests.

It's Due Tomorrow!

Carrie's social studies teacher was interesting, creative, and bright. She also gave out tons of homework and very involved projects that needed to be completed in a short period of time. It was not unusual for Carrie to have an hour's worth of social studies every night, on top of her other homework. But the last straw was when a project was assigned the week of Thanksgiving.

"She gave it to us on Tuesday," said Carrie. "We had to build a model and turn in a written report as well. She said it wasn't due for ten days, but anyone who turned it in on Monday, after Thanksgiving break, would get extra credit. We had relatives coming down for Thanksgiving dinner that I hadn't seen in a while, but I spent most of the holiday working on the project. My mother was angry."

Big loads of homework over weekends and holidays rate high on the "unfair work habits" list. While kids realize that homework is part of school, many wondered why teachers couldn't coordinate their workloads better.

"Don't teachers talk to each other?" asked Josie, fifteen. "Some days, I can have a half-hour of homework and then other days, each teacher loads us down as though that was the only class we have. Then they all schedule tests for the same day. If it was spaced out better, we could study better and learn more."

But what if you turn in your work and the teacher won't look at it, repeatedly loses work, or even worse — throws it away, like Kurt's teacher? What's a kid to do when faced with a situation he or she feels is unfair?

A PLAN FOR SURVIVAL

Anytime you plan to take on "the boss," you had better first get your facts straight and have a positive alternate plan organized if you hope to make any points. Trying to survive an unfair teacher is no exception.

Begin with a Reality Check. Specifically, what is the problem as you see it? Is it that you feel picked on? That the teacher doesn't answer questions or give help when needed? Or is it that the teacher plays favorites? Figure out how you specifically are affected. Then, part of the Reality Check in this case is to ask others if they have the same opinion.

This doesn't mean that you rush to your lunch table and say, "I hate Mrs. Cranberry because she's mean, rotten, and unfair. What do you think?" You approach a friend and say, "When Mrs. Cranberry gives tests, her directions are so unclear that I give wrong answers because I don't know what she's asking. Do you feel that way?" Or, "When Mrs. Cranberry screams at me in front of the class, it makes me feel like crying. I get so upset, I can't concentrate for the rest of the period. Has that ever happened to you?"

Sometimes others will have experienced the same situation. You may find that what *you* interpret as unfair, others may just view as a demanding teacher, or they may not have been in your situation. Sometimes an "unfair teacher" charge is only a personality conflict between the teacher and student and when that happens, you may view everything that teacher does or says as rotten, just because you don't like his or her personality.

If you determine that the problem is something that *is* a situation that needs changing, you Take a Positive Risk and look at your options.

I spoke not only to students about this subject, but to a number of counselors and teachers as well. They all agreed that communication is necessary, but you have to plan it out carefully. One teacher told me, "It's difficult to criticize another teacher's methods. If the student is really being affected in a negative way, though, or is missing material because of it, something should definitely be said."

You can do this one of several ways. If you find that *you* are the one with the problem (such as being picked on), you can approach the teacher yourself. If you feel that you need help, you can find an advocate—someone who will speak for you—in either your parent, counselor, or other adult whom you trust. If you find that the teacher's actions are affecting the entire class or a group of students (prejudice against boys or girls or unclear directions), you might select three representatives to approach the teacher.

In any case, ask the teacher for a meeting time when you can talk privately. Whether it is *your* problem or the *group's* problem, no teacher will listen to criticism in front of a class. Even if that teacher has humiliated *you* by screaming at you in public, you should request a private meeting.

"My English teacher, who is kind of bossy, marked one of my right answers wrong on a test and then discussed why it was wrong in front of the class. I knew it was right but I kept my mouth shut," said Karen. "After class, I went up to her and showed her that she had made a mistake and why. She was quiet and I thought she would get mad at me but she said, 'You're right' and changed it."

Cool Communication in this case means you don't attack teachers. Rather you explain how *their* specific actions made you *feel*. For example:

You: "Mrs. Cranberry, when you scream at me in front of the class, I get very upset and embarrassed. I know that I make mistakes, but could you tell me in private?"

Mrs. Cranberry: "I didn't realize you felt that way. I just have a loud personality. I have to point out errors in class because it would take too much time to speak with each student individually. But if there's anything major that's wrong, I'll talk to you in private. OK?"

"You have to keep your cool and don't scream," said Adam, twelve, "even though that's what you feel like doing. Because then it will just be worse on you. Then they'll take it out on you for the rest of the year."

Celie, fifteen, agrees. "You have to keep your voice calm. Instead of saying 'You did this!' you can say 'You probably don't realize it, but . . .'"

Several students said that if they thought the teacher could not be approached, they would try to get another teacher involved indirectly.

"You can tell others about the incident when another teacher is listening — and you know they're listening but you're acting like you don't know," said Jim, thirteen. "You can't call the teacher names or anything, but you can say how upset you were. Then you just hope for the best."

An important aspect of communicating to a teacher is to offer a positive alternative. You can't just tell them what you feel without offering a solution. For example:

"Mrs. Cranberry, instead of giving us so much homework over the weekend, could you give us an assignment on Monday and make it due on Friday?"

A Reality Check of the situation will tell you two things overall. First, sometimes approaching a teacher will work and sometimes it won't. Second, you will have that teacher for a finite period of time — not for the rest of your life! If you Take a Positive Risk and attempt to "right a wrong" and it doesn't work — don't give up. Believe it or not, you will have grown from the experience and be better able to handle a similar situation in the future.

PART FOUR

BOY/GIRL RELATIONSHIPS

Chapter 13

Who is this Alien?

"A boy I liked asked 'Do you want me to kiss you?' and when I said yes, he screamed 'Sweat alert!' and went off laughing to his friends! It was so embarrassing. Why do boys act so stupid?" (Sharon, 12)

"Us guys were having a towel fight in the locker room and when I looked down, I had gotten a hard-on. Some of the other guys noticed it too. A couple laughed and pointed and said 'Watch out! He must be a fag.' I never thought I was gay. Did that mean I was gay?" (Leon, 13)

"I was at the department store alone buying a bra. When I went to pick mine out, all the rest in the display fell down on me. Then when I went to pay for it, the cash register was closed and I was told to go pay in the boy's section. When I got there, there was a boy about 16 running the cash register. I stuffed the bra under some shirts on a counter and left!" (Jennifer, 14)

Sometimes it seems more like a nightmare than a wonderful miracle.

You rise from your bed and look in the mirror at yourself and Yikes! There's someone staring back at you who has hair sticking out in odd places, has red bumps growing larger and larger, and may sound croaky and unnatural.

At school, you notice that even kids you have known since kindergarten are getting funny-looking as well as looking at you differently. Girls herd together giggling and pointing and sticking all kinds of grease and powder on their faces. Boys move in packs that are loud and sometimes physically violent — pushing, shoving and tripping. Both the boys and girls try to watch the other when they think no one is noticing. If and when they *have* to come in contact, some actually shake, drop things, and stutter as though they had forgotten how to talk! Has everyone suddenly gone crazy? Have you and your friends been replaced by "pod people"?

Just who are these aliens, anyway?

One of the most exciting changes that occurs at this point in your life is the change in your relationship with members of the opposite sex. This change can make you feel one moment like you're walking on a cloud and in the next, feel as though you are walking a tightrope high above the crowd with only hungry lions below, waiting for you to fall! Those hormones that are beginning to rush through your body not only create a lot of physical changes over which you have no control, but changes in your feelings as well. Combine those changes with the fact that you are facing new situations and you might feel like one thirteen-year-old girl did who said, "Sometimes I feel like Dr. Jekyll and Mr. Hyde. My body does things without my telling it to. My feelings get all twisted up and make me want to cry. I feel like nobody knows the real me. Sometimes I wish I was a kid again." Looking back to days when you could play with other kids your parents picked out for you, bopping them on the head with a Nerf brick if you got angry, and then sharing a Popsicle whether it was a Judy or a Jim makes today look pretty complicated. Back then, it didn't really matter whether you played with a boy or a girl. What you talked about centered on what you were doing—building, playing with Play-Doh, watching "Sesame Street." Thoughts turned towards food, picking on your brother or sister, and learning about the world around you.

You are still learning about the world, but now it does make a difference whether you are hanging out with boys or girls. Talking to them no longer seems simple. In fact, most of those who were surveyed said that they found the opposite sex confusing.

Top Three Comments From . . .	
Girls about Boys	**Boys about Girls**
1. Why do boys act so silly and immature around us?	1. Why do girls act so silly and giggly around us?
2. Why do boys act friendly in private and then pretend they don't know you in front of their friends?	2. What do girls think and talk about?
3. What do boys think and talk about?	3. Why do girls have to get so serious?

As you might be able to see from these comments, everyone is facing the same type of confusion. What do you talk about? What is the other person thinking and how should I act? Can I be myself and still have boys/girls like me?

You are, in many ways, like an actor in a new play. You are still *you* underneath, but your costume may be different from your everyday clothing and there are new ways to move, new cues to learn, and other actors to deal with. When a new play opens, even the most professional actors are nervous, uncertain, and jittery because they are new to the role. As the play runs for several years, the role becomes a part of the actor who no longer has to think so hard about it. He or she just faces the audience and performs. Sure, they might feel a little nervous as the curtain opens, but once they get started, they become comfortable.

You are now growing into new roles. Your costume — your body — is also growing into a new, more adult form and it will take some time to get used to. Even moving, talking, and relating to others is new in this respect. Of course you are a little confused and uncertain. You have a right to be!

The good news is this will pass as you become more comfortable with your new self and have practiced being with others. But there are many factors around us that contribute to your uncertainty, and you have to stop and Do a Reality Check in order to spot them.

The Reality of Your Body

Did you ever play with Barbie or GI Joe dolls?

Barbie is always perfect. Her hair flows, her breasts are large, her stomach is flat, and her clothes would be the envy of any fashion model. GI Joe and his friends are also perfect. Big muscular torsos, flat stomachs, and rugged faces. Neither doll sweats at the wrong time or gets body odor, body hair, or pimples. They are the ideal person at his or her best. There is no way any of us can measure up to that. And dolls aren't the only ones around that influence our ideas.

Approximately 80% of young people say they learn about relationships from television and magazines. Think about the television and magazine ads you see each day. People with perfect hair and perfect teeth. Even ads for diarrhea and pimple creams show smiling perfect people. Television ads or programs don't show the humiliation and worry of a girl who might get her first menstrual period on the school bus and not realize it until she gets up to leave. Then her friends point out the stain on her skirt—and sometimes in a mean and teasing way.

"One boy yelled 'Hey, you been sitting in a bucket of red paint or are you bleeding?' The whole bus heard him!" said one thirteen year old.

You also don't see on commercials a boy trying to control a body that seems to have a mind of its own. His voice is unsteady, his penis gets hard at the most embarrassing times — and it may have nothing at all to do with females, homosexuality, or sex at all. One boy said that it seemed his penis hardened when he got embarrassed by anything. It could happen when he was in the locker room with the boys or in front of math class when he goofed up a problem on the blackboard.

Remember how we talked in Chapter One about how unreal it is to judge yourself in comparison to an adult at this point in your life because you are still a house under construction? Most young people also compare their bodies to those ideals that they have known since childhood — Barbie, GI Joe, and all the models on television and in magazines. Not only are you comparing yourself to "finished" adults, but to unreal ones as well. Very few people in the world look that perfect. In fact, even the lovely Christie Brinkley (who many girls mentioned) said in a magazine interview once that she was always self-conscious when she wore a bathing suit in public because people expected her to look like she does in magazine photos. What people didn't realize, however, was that those photos took a lot of posing and angle changing so her body *would* look perfect, whether it was or not!

When asked to describe their bodies, very few kids had anything complimentary to say. Whether boy or girl, the most frequent answers were: Too fat, too muscular, short, chunky, sweaty, clunky knees, hairy, and puny. Girls often said "flat" or "boobs too big" and boys would mention "undersized" or "too skinny." Very few used more complimentary phrases like: slender, nice looking, pretty, or "good but not great."

With everyone walking around focusing on the negative aspects of their changing bodies — and thinking that everyone else is focusing on it too — no wonder it's difficult to speak when a member of the opposite sex approaches.

Do a Reality Check. This is a time of change and change means new situations. Just as each person is different in looks, each is different in growth patterns as well. Some of that is inherited and some is individual. For example, if you are a boy and your father or mother went through puberty at a very young age (nine), then it is very likely that you will begin to change physically at a younger age than most of your friends. If you find yourself behind your friends in development, don't worry—it will happen.

Cool Communication is called for in many of these new situations. Remember that most young people said that they valued kindness as a trait in friends. It is particularly important to be kind when one of your peers is struggling with his or her body changes. Rather than taunt, tease, and make jokes, you may find that a kind word of understanding will come back to you when *you* need it. You are not alone in your uncertainties or embarrassments and it helps to let a friend know.

It also helps to know that boys and girls at this stage are developing differently, not only physically but emotionally as well. This adds to those feelings that the person you are trying to talk to just landed from Ork and decided to wear spaghetti as a hat.

Boys and Girls are Different

Twelve-year-old Cindy wanted to get Jason to notice her. She had known Jason since fourth grade but only recently had noticed that he had a really nice smile and clear green eyes. He would smile and say "Hi!" in the halls but whenever she tried to talk to him, he'd just scurry off. "Uh, gotta go now. See ya!" he'd say. So Cindy formed a plan.

She decided to have a party. That way she could invite Jason to something outside of school. Since she would be the hostess and the hostess usually gets a lot of attention, he would be sure to notice her. Unfortunately, it didn't quite turn out the way Cindy had hoped.

Cindy and her friends took great care to pick just the right outfits for the party. They spent several hours decorating the basement with balloons and streamers. Cindy's parents had gotten just what Cindy wanted for refreshments — chips, pretzels, pizza, soda, and ice cream for "make your own" sundaes.

While some of the kids danced as a group, most of the girls wound up standing around talking to each other and eyeing the boys while the boys stuffed themselves with chips and pretzels, pizza and ice cream. Jason was no different.

At the end of the party, the boys said "Cindy, it was a great party!" and meant it. The girls filed out more quietly.

What happened? Just as young people develop at different rates physically, boys and girls also develop at different rates emotionally. The reality is that often the girls are maturing to the point where they are full of romantic dreams and warm feelings first. At this point, though, many boys are still more interested in dirt bikes, rockets, skateboarding, and eating. And this is reflected in what they talk about.

The girls, when they get together, talk about boys. What kinds of boys attract them, whom they like, and why they like them. Of course there are other things — teachers, future career plans, and who's getting their ears pierced, but "boys" is a major topic. Since many boys are not yet that interested in the girls, the girls might substitute rock singers or television or movie stars as their "dream men" and talk about them.

The boys may talk about girls, but more to comment on them physically rather than in a romantic way. Then they move on to "more important" topics like paintball guns, sports, movies, skateboarding, or dirt bikes.

By the time they reach thirteen or fourteen, though, both boys and girls are noticing each other in a big way and trying to figure out what to do with all these new feelings of attraction. They are also trying to figure out what to do with all these strange feelings their bodies are experiencing.

One of those "strange feelings" that is new to your body is often whispered about, joked about, and sometimes thought to be "bad" or unnatural.

GETTING TO KNOW YOURSELF

Do you think it's wrong to touch your neck or your knee? How about your stomach? How about your own genitals?

Most people would say "No" to the first two questions, but be unsure about the last one. Why? Because you have been taught that it is wrong for others to touch you in your "private places." Does that mean that touching yourself in your "private places" is wrong?

This gets more confusing because you may find that touching or rubbing your clitoris or penis actually feels very good — a new feeling for your body. In fact, it might feel so good that you become sexually excited to the point of orgasm or sexual release. This activity — masturbation — has been the point of much discussion and misinformation and teaching through centuries.

Because it has to do with sexual feelings and release rather than reproduction, many in some religions were fearful that it was wrong, unnatural, or would make a person go crazy. You may even have heard jokes about some guy checking to see if he has "hair growing in the palm of his hand" — another myth about masturbation. One girl even wrote me that "I used to masturbate but that was before I became real religious. Now I've stopped."

Your body *is* private and others touching you in a way that makes you uncomfortable *is* wrong. But touching your own body and feeling good is not wrong and it has nothing to do with religion. It is natural for you to want to see what these feelings are like and how your own body responds. There's nothing dirty about your body — it is a wonderful creation. Take a look at it and know what it can do.

What does this have to do with boy/girl relationships? Very simply, in order for you to learn how to view others and relationships in a healthy way, you must first realize your own value. This means having a good attitude as well as knowledge about your own body.

Some of you may have had Family Life classes in school which have answered your questions. Whether you do or don't have those classes, you can go to your parents or another adult you feel comfortable talking with, to answer any questions you might have concerning the changes that are going on in your body right now and how your body works.

If you understand that what you have is a kind of miracle machine that can perform great feats and bring you pleasure, then perhaps you will stop and Do a Reality Check about letting it be used by others. Feeling attracted romantically and sexually towards members of the opposite sex is natural and is Nature's way of continuing the race of human beings. Sex is the physical side of that relationship and is often the side that gets everyone's attention. But sex is not how you form a friendship or get to know someone.

You start by feeling good about yourself and then learning to express those feelings you have towards others in a healthy way. Like everything else in your life right now, learning to express those feelings sometimes takes a different turn than you expected.

CHAPTER 14

HEAD-BUTTING AND OTHER LOVE PATS

Jack had had it with Melissa. For the last two weeks, she would come up to him, punch him in the arm and laughingly run away. When he told his parents, they said, "Oh, I guess she likes you!"

"Likes me? Are you crazy? She's nothing but a pain," Jack retorted. "If she likes me, she sure has a dumb way of showing it!"

Dealing with these new feelings of liking a member of the opposite sex can be very confusing. What do you say to him or her? You don't want to sound like a jerk. And what if you get rejected? That would be embarrassing and you'll feel stupid.

So you look at the person you secretly have a crush on and try to figure out what to do. In your head, you're cool, calm, and eloquent. You could be saying "You have the brightest blue eyes I've ever seen and I'd like to talk to you."

But your body gets the message, scrambles it up, and says, "OK, I'll stomp on his foot."

Uh-oh. You don't exactly get the reaction you had hoped for. Part of the problem may be that many people feel they have to act differently around members of the opposite sex.

"I always feel as though I have to smile more," said Carla, thirteen.

"I try to be a little more cool, more macho," said Jose, twelve.

"I try to use a better vocabulary, but that doesn't always work out," said Bill, fourteen. "I was trying to sound intelligent and used the wrong words to describe something and one of the girls in the group pointed it out in front of everybody and they all laughed."

It *is* embarrassing to make the first move, to try to impress or to try to express new feelings and then be rejected or look like a fool. This can be avoided, though, and your real self and feelings can shine through.

First you start with a Reality Check. What is it you feel? Attraction.

What is it you want? To tell the person you are crazy about him or her and get their attention. What are your options? Think about it. Here are some that tend to get the opposite reaction.

Oh, No! Not Him Again!

"Every time I went to get a drink of water before English, this boy Jeff would come up behind me and push my face in the water," said Bonnie. "Why do boys act so dumb?"

"They were heavily into pulling pants down at my school last year," said Martha. "This one guy I know, Vic, got mine down in the middle of the hallway. I had liked him before, but not after that!"

"There's this girl, Terry, who always takes my books out of my desk," said Todd. "Then she makes me ask for them back at least twenty times. She giggles the whole time. I can't stand her!"

Poor Jeff, Terry, and Vic. They were probably trying to say, "I like you! Notice me!" They got noticed, all right, but not exactly the way they wanted. Instead of Todd, Martha, and Bonnie thinking "Oh, he (she) likes me," they think "This person can't stand me and wants to annoy me."

Other options of getting attention that work equally as badly include head-butting ("This is big in my school and I hate it!" said one sixth grader), name-calling ("This girl keeps calling me 'Tree' because I'm tall and I can't stand it!"), and poking. ("The boys come up behind you and take their fingers and poke you in both sides. I've dropped all my books a few times and it's a real pain!" said a seventh grader.)

None of these options involve Cool Communication. Neither does violent action, which some boys seem to think is "manly." Hitting, grabbing a girl by the hair, or making demands on someone does not show affection. What it does show is that the person who is this aggressive has a major problem and needs professional help. Those problems are serious and cannot be helped by the simple kindness of a friend or girlfriend.

So what is a person to do? You *could* just talk to the boy or girl you like . . . but wait. There's one more option before *that* scary one — the Crab Approach.

MOVE LIKE A CRAB

Have you ever watched a crab scurry along the water's edge as it heads for a safe sand hole? It doesn't approach the hole by walking directly to it. It moves sideways, kind of in a zigzag pattern. It may even pass the hole once before it actually runs into it.

Sometimes when a person likes somebody but doesn't know how to tell her, he uses the "crab approach" — that is, he tries to let her know in a sideways fashion by letting a friend tell her. Sometimes the friend is recruited for this job. Sometimes the friend decides to get involved without being asked. This can result in two people being embarrassed instead of one.

"Just as I was walking into the cafeteria, my friend told this girl that I really liked her," said Andy, twelve. "I did, but I wasn't going to tell her that way. She just kind of looked at me and got red."

Even family members can get into the act.

"My brother, who is two years older than me, had some friends over, including Bryan who he knew I liked for a long time (but Bryan didn't know it)," said Audrey, fourteen. "I came downstairs to ask a question and all the boys started walking past me upstairs and one guy said, 'Well, I guess you'll want to stay down here and smooch with Bryan. We all know you looove him.' My face got so red, I ran back upstairs and hit my brother."

Brad, thirteen, also found how getting other people involved can mess things up.

"There's this kid named Brad who sits next to me in Home Ec," said Celia. "Over school vacation, his friend called me and asked if I'd like to go out with Brad. I said 'maybe' but why didn't he ask me himself. His friend said that Brad thought this was a better way, so I told him I'd tell him when we got back to school.

"For two weeks after we got back in school, all my friends told me that Brad talked about me all the time. I wrote my friend Diane a note about Brad. It said:

'Hi Diane! So how's your life? English class is very boring. I am not going to go out with Brad. That's final! He's sort of weird, if you know what I mean! See U at lunch. Hopefully, Greg, Scott, and Brad won't come over again. Bye! Write Back!'

"Well, Greg and Scott came over to our lunch table and saw the note in Diane's assignment book and said they were going to have some fun with it. Now every day in band practice, one of my friends goes up to Brad and tells him I like him. He turns totally red."

When a friend gets involved in expressing your feelings for you, these are the possible results:

1. The person you like may wind up liking the one who's speaking for you.
2. He/she may think you're weird for not talking to them directly.
3. He/she may decide they like you, but following your example, may hold back from talking to you.
4. He/she could decide they like you and talk to you — but then you still have to talk with them directly anyway.

When you consider all the possibilities, doesn't it make more sense to take control of the situation and get your feelings across in a positive way?

Take a Positive Risk!

No one likes to feel rejected. It doesn't matter whether you are a boy or a girl, thirteen or thirty. Being rejected makes you feel bad about yourself. It is the fear of being rejected that so often keeps people — especially young people who are just beginning to feel attractions — from expressing how they actually feel. But there are a few tricks you can use to ease into those situations.

Remember Jack and Melissa from the beginning of the chapter? Instead of punching Jack's arm to get his attention, it could have been handled this way:

Melissa: Jack, that's a great shirt you're wearing. It really brings out the color in your eyes.
Jack (feeling pleased): Thank you! Are you going to math class now?

If Melissa had Taken a Positive Risk and actually talked to Jack and paid him a compliment, it could have started a nice friendship. Paying someone an honest compliment is a great way to begin a discussion or to let someone else know that you like them. They will be flattered that you took the time to notice *them* and say something. No one rejects a person who is paying them a compliment. Can you imagine the conversation going this way?

Melissa: Jack, that's a great shirt you're wearing. It really brings out the color in your eyes.
Jack: Melissa, you're such a jerk. Anyone could see I look terrible.

That conversation is highly unlikely. Everyone has something worth complimenting every day and would love it if someone else noticed. Very often we hear what is wrong about us. It is not only wonderful to hear what is right, but we tend to like the person who noticed!

So Taking a Positive Risk and paying an honest compliment is the first step to expressing your feelings.

Second, look at the person you like as a *person* and find out about them. That may sound pretty simple, but it's something that many of us forget. Jeff may have thought Bonnie had the prettiest hair he had ever seen on a girl, but Bonnie is more than just hair. She is a person with likes, dislikes, and feelings about things. To get Bonnie's attention, Jeff would push her face in the water fountain. Here's how he could have gotten different results.

Jeff (To Bonnie who is getting a drink of water): Hi, Bonnie. You know, your hair always looks so nice.
Bonnie (flattered): Thank you! Well, it's time for good old English class.
Jeff: Yeah. Which is *your* favorite class?

And then Bonnie would answer and Jeff could tell her what *he* likes to do. This opens the door to talk about other interests. The key word here is *talk*. That is the foundation for a good friendship. What do you talk about to a boy or a girl? The same kinds of things that make *you* interesting. You can talk about things you have in common: school, teachers, school events, or activities. You can ask questions to get to know him/her as a person.

For example, asking "favorites" is a good way to get a conversation going and find out about the person at the same time. What is your favorite: food, color, animal, vacation, class, teacher, music group? etc. Then follow it up with a couple more questions: Why is

. . . your favorite? How does it make you feel?

Before you know it, you'll be talking about things that are important to you like goals, future plans, and even your families. These are all topics that are common to both boys and girls and you don't have to do any "homework" (like reading up on a particular sport or rock group) in order to discuss it.

The person you speak to will get the message:

"He/she likes me because he/she is asking me questions about myself. I must be important to him/her. That's a nice feeling."

Now you're getting the attention you want in a positive way. You are getting the point across: "I like you a lot!" And you may find that in addition to a good "talking" friendship, you may want to express those feelings of affection with something more physical.

FROM FRIENDSHIP TO ROMANCE

One of the wonderful things about being a human being is that we not only have feelings of love and caring, but we can show those feelings in a huge variety of ways. No other creature has this ability.

Some mammals that are more advanced might show affection, but they cannot speak. They go from sniffing each other to mating and reproducing. Only humans can show we care about someone in ways that are both verbal and physical without the final step of mating (or sex).

Part of what you are learning at this stage of your life is what you like in a person and what you don't like. This is so that, at some point in the future, you can select a mate who you feel will be right for you. How you go about gathering this information is by falling "in love" with a number of different people before the right one comes along.

Loving someone outside your family is a wonderful and scary feeling because it's a different kind of love than you have felt before. You can love your parents or a special teacher or friend, but you don't walk around thinking about them all the time. When you find yourself loving someone romantically, not only your thoughts and heart get involved but you also find that your body is getting involved as well.

For example, when Nancy and Jimmy were eight years old and Nancy handed Jimmy an orange and their hands touched, all they felt was skin touching skin. Now they are older and Nancy finds that she feels romantic towards Jimmy. If their hands touch even accidentally, she feels something like a tingling or an electrical shock. She may also get a warm "turned on" feeling. Amazing! Not only that but Jimmy, who also cares for Nancy, might find that his body is also reacting and tingling.

These changes are normal and natural. At some point in the future, when you are with the person you want to make a commitment to, these changes prepare your body for sexual intercourse. But just because your body responds now doesn't mean you should have sex. In fact, there are many reasons why you should not. Some of these will be discussed over the next two chapters, but the one that applies here is that many people think sex is the only way to show affection for someone else. This is not true.

When I asked middle schoolers how they show affection for members of the opposite sex, I got a variety of answers.

"I hug and kiss my boyfriend."

"We hold hands."

"I talk on the telephone to my girlfriend for hours."

"We eat lunch together."

"My boyfriend and I tell each other how great we think the other person is."

"I buy my girlfriend her favorite gum."

"I always call to say goodnight."

These are all specific and healthy ways of showing love for another person. There are many more which include making or writing something for the person you love, sharing events and doing things that will make the other person happy — like letting them pick the movie to see, being kind to their siblings, and respecting their feelings. You don't always have to agree with them, just show respect for them.

But I also got this response from some middle schoolers when I asked how they show affection.

"We have a sexual relationship." (an eighth grader)

"I show I care by agreeing to have sex with my boyfriend."

Different studies of middle schoolers report that anywhere from 20% to 55% of adolescents from sixth to ninth grades have had sexual intercourse. Reports also say that this is because many middle schoolers see sex as a sign of affection.

Having a sexual relationship with someone, however, is much more than a simple expression of caring. It is a demand for a commitment of both mind and body. It is a deep communication between people who are mature enough to be good friends and who want to share a part of life together. It involves serious responsibilities such as birth control and faithfulness to one person. It is not used to "join the club" or "prove how much you love me, baby."

SEX IS NOT A SIMPLE LOVE PAT

It is tempting to think that what goes on inside your head should go on outside your body. In your head, you can imagine what it is like to make love with someone you care about. But *thinking* something and *doing* something are two completely different things. There are no consequences to thinking. There are consequences to actions.

Your bodies may respond physically to the attraction you feel for each other — and *you* may think about having sex — but you are in control of your body. You can use your brain to Do a Reality Check and look at your options, just like Nancy and Jimmy had to do.

Touching each other felt so good that Jimmy felt a tension building up inside of him. He told Nancy, "If you really love me and want to make me happy, you'll make love with me. You know I love you."

Nancy was tempted because she really loved Jimmy and had imagined what it would be like. She also felt a tension building up when they touched each other but she first Did a Reality Check.

1. Nancy was fourteen years old. She had many years of education and dating ahead of her before she wanted the responsibilities of a sexual relationship.

2. She loved Jimmy today, but what about next year or even next month? Her likes and dislikes changed frequently these days since she was being exposed to new experiences.

3. Once you have sex with someone, that act follows you for the rest of your entire life. You cannot take it back or forget it. She wasn't sure that at fourteen she wanted to start carrying around the names of people she had had sex with.

4. She felt she would die if her parents found out. Her family val-

ues and church upbringing said to wait until she was older and more sure of herself.

5. She didn't want word to get around school that she was "sleeping" with her boyfriend.

6. Just thinking about getting involved in a sexual relationship was complicating her life. She had her hands full just trying to make good grades in school and keep up with her music lessons.

7. She did care about Jimmy and didn't want to make him unhappy.

This was a tough decision for Nancy, especially since the boy she cared about was asking her to do something that was supposed to feel good. Since there was a lot to think about, Nancy decided to write down her realities and options on a piece of paper so she could look at them in black and white. She made two columns on the paper and headed them "Action" and "Possible Results."

Action	Possible Result
Have sex with Jimmy	Pregnancy; disease; guilt; feel rejected and hurt when relationship ends; damage to reputation; conflicts with parents if they find out; Options: Try to cope
Tell Jimmy, "No, I'm not ready for that"	Losing Jimmy as a boyfriend; Options: Show love in other ways like spending time together doing sports and school activities; dances; kissing and cuddling, etc.

Nancy knew that she was risking losing Jimmy if she said no but she also knew that she didn't want the unhealthy results that having sex would bring at fourteen years old. She decided to Take a Positive Risk for herself and say "No" but suggest the other options.

She used Cool Communication when talking with Jimmy. She didn't attack him — she told him how she felt about him and how she felt about herself.

Jimmy (Sitting in the dark basement with his arms around her): Did you think about us and what I asked you?

Nancy (Taking a deep breath): Yes I did. I thought about it a lot. Jimmy, I just can't do it. I can't make love with you.

Jimmy (Feeling rejected): I thought you loved me!

Nancy: I do love you!

Jimmy: Then prove it! You know I love you.

Nancy: Jimmy, having sex with you doesn't prove I love you. It just proves I can do it. I'm just not ready for that kind of relationship, yet. There's lots of other ways we can prove our love for each other. (She lists the options.) Those things take time and caring — that's what proves love.

Jimmy: Don't I turn you on? You turn me on!

Nancy: Of course you do. But I told you, I'm not ready for sex yet. You don't have to agree with me but if you really care about me, you'll respect my feelings.

Jimmy (Feeling let down and irritated): Okay, we can try it your way for awhile, but I'm not promising anything. I guess we'd better go back upstairs if we're not going to do anything.

The funny thing about Jimmy's reaction is that he may act *irritated* but could actually be *relieved*. Boys, more than girls, feel the pressure to "make a move." The pressure may come from movies, magazines, or peers.

"Hey, get real," said one fifteen-year-old boy. "It seems like if you don't try something with a girl, she and your friends think you're a fag. So you try. It doesn't mean that you really are ready for something like a sexual relationship, but at least you don't look queer."

If you look at the ways in which you can show a boy or girl that you care about them, you might see a range like this:

Stomping on foot • • • Hug/Kiss/Handholding/Activities/etc. • • • Sex

The items at both ends are not proofs of affection. The activities in between are. Those are what make up a real and caring relationship between boys and girls, men and women. Those are the "love pats" that everyone needs and enjoys.

CHAPTER 15

DATE?
WHAT'S A DATE?

Fifteen-year-old Deedee and her friends usually wind up meeting at one of the girls' or boys' homes to watch videos and eat pizza on Saturday nights.

Twelve-year-olds Greg and Lisa meet and eat lunch together at school three afternoons a week.

Paul and Clare, both thirteen, go to Clare's empty apartment after school two afternoons a week to have sex.

And Michelle, fourteen, and Michael, fifteen, get a ride over to the bowling alley and then walk to the nearby mall afterwards.

Each of these kids calls his or her activity a "date." What do *you* think a date is?

Strictly speaking, Webster's dictionary defines a date as "a social engagement between two people of the opposite sex." But there are a lot of other meanings as well. Cindy might say she has a date to go shopping with Susan; Bill might say he has a date to play tennis with Sam. Both of those are dates, even though they are activities with members of the same sex.

When Big Bird said he had a date with Maria, he usually meant that they were going to Mr. Hooper's store for a soda. When your grandmother said she had a date, she might have meant that a young man was coming over to have supper under the watchful eye of your great-grandfather. And when two characters from a soap opera say they have a date, it often means that they are going to wind up in bed together.

It's no wonder then that four out of five adolescents whom I've surveyed said they needed more information on dating behavior and what a date really is. It didn't matter whether the kids were eleven or sixteen—the confusion was the same.

One of the things you've probably been looking forward to as you reach adolescence and your teen years is dating. Some of your ideas about dating may have come from your parents, and some of your ideas may have come from older brothers and sisters or friends. Still other ideas about dating today come from television and movies—and this can be dangerous to you.

What a Date is Not

Just as Barbie and GI Joe are unreal as role models, so are the characters on television and in movies. Soap operas are the worst at showing what relationships between real people are like, yet they are often the most copied by young people.

According to people who keep statistics on this sort of thing, the average length of time on a television show between two people meeting and then falling into a sexual relationship with each other is eight and one-half minutes. Do a Reality Check! This is not real life! Television people rarely worry about getting sexually transmitted diseases, getting pregnant (unless it adds to the drama), becoming depressed and hurt when the relationship is over, or the responsibilities of a long-term relationship.

Flip through a magazine and you might see two people in an ad trying to sell jeans. Are they running around doing errands, riding a horse, going to a ball game, or skateboarding? *That* is what *real* people do when they wear jeans to be comfortable. The advertisers instead have chosen to show two people, naked from the waist up touching each other in a way that would lead you to believe that they are getting ready to take off the rest of their clothing.

After being surrounded with the unreal images on television, in movies, and in advertising, many young people have the idea that a "date" is the same thing as "having sex." This is wrong and untrue. This is not your fault, but rather the fault of the adults in the media and those who allow it to continue.

Because of the bad information young people are getting, there are many who shy away from dating because they just don't know what to expect and they don't want to have sex.

There's Safety in Numbers

"Oh, nobody dates anymore. We just kinda go around in a

group," said Kit, sixteen.

"When there's a group of kids together, we can have fun and there's no pressure," said Lucy, thirteen.

"There's not a whole lot to do for kids around here," said Armando, fourteen. "When we get together, we have a little beer, maybe other stuff. Then we walk around and go home."

When a group of kids gets together to have a good time, that used to be called a party. Today, the words "party" and "date" are almost interchangeable. Oh, there are still birthday parties or parties to celebrate a special event, but there are also gatherings of eight or more kids to watch videos, dance to a DJ and music, or go to the movies.

Since, as an adolescent, you cannot get a driver's license, you have to depend upon parents for transportation to and from a party or date. For this reason, many kids said they would rather just stay home and get a few kids to come over to their house. Sometimes they would plan something, sometimes not. Sometimes this wound up getting them into trouble because they saw their choices of activities as: television, videos, drinking, drugs, or sex — or maybe a combination of some of those. The fewer the people, the more possibilities for trouble.

"I enjoy going out with a group of friends that I like," said Lucy. "I don't really have a boyfriend. I would love to have one but I don't think I'm ready for sex. There are guys I like as friends, and my girlfriends and I and the guys get together and watch a tape and then have something to eat. Maybe we'll play kissing games."

Kit also feels there's a certain safety in numbers. "Sometimes we'll start off as a group and then some kids pair off by themselves. Kids don't 'date around' anymore — they just 'see' one person. When that's over, they 'see' another person. Sex is usually part of what's expected. If you date around, people say you're a tramp."

A girl used to be called a tramp if she went around having sex with a number of partners. The only way this word applies to dating a number of boys is if you think a "date" equals "sex." Dating and sex are *not* the same thing. You can date a number of people and enjoy fun activities without being a "tramp."

Between meeting a person of the opposite sex and having a

sexual relationship, there should be a great deal of activity, events, and shared experiences. This is all part of dating. The television and movies don't show this to you because it takes *time* and time is something that is very expensive when you're in the TV or movie business. So they show you the beginning and they show you the end—all in one-half hour!

Do a Reality Check! You *have* time. That's what being an adolescent is all about—time to change, time to learn, time to grow as a person, and time to figure out what makes different kinds of relationships work.

"But," said Armando, "where are we gonna learn what to do?"

There are several options, but you can begin right here.

Red Light, Green Light —Go!

Did you ever play the game Red Light, Green Light?

In this game, one person is "It" and stands with his back turned towards the others. When he says "Green Light," everyone else starts to quickly sneak up on him. When he yells "Red Light," he spins around. Everyone has to stop quickly because if the person who's "It" sees you move, you're out of the game. The winner is the first person to get to "It" without being caught moving.

Dating behavior can be broken down into a game of Red Light, Green Light. There are certain things that are fun to do with one or a group of people. We can call these activities Green Light behaviors. You can "Go" without worry and enjoy yourself.

Then there are Yellow Light behaviors and activities. If you find yourself engaged in these, slow down because there is danger ahead. This danger could be physical or emotional. In either case, Yellow Light activities will make you feel uncertain, perhaps guilty, and maybe scared.

Finally, there are Red Light behaviors. You should stop when confronted with these activities. Freeze — do not move forward. These are the activities that are wrong, are against the law, or signal situations you are not capable of handling. They can cause you pain and guilt and affect your life in a negative way—possibly forever.

Take a look.

GREEN LIGHT BEHAVIORS FOR DATES

- Going to movies
- Watching sporting events
- Playing sports — Bowling, Miniature Golf, Ice Skating, Skiing, Swimming, etc.
- Playing board games at home (You learn a lot about a person when you play a board game with him/her!)
- Watching videos or television
- Dances and parties
- School events
- Any activities that take place in public — like a concert in the park or arena; a flea market or shopping mall, etc.
- Kissing and hugging
- Holding hands
- Putting your arm around someone

YELLOW LIGHT BEHAVIORS—BE CAREFUL, DANGER AHEAD!

- Putting your hands under your date's clothing
- Heavy Petting — touching the breasts or genitals of your partner to excite him/her sexually
- Losing your temper
- Extreme bossiness or demands
- Sitting in the back seat of a darkened car
- Going to your partner's house when no parent or sibling is at home
- Inviting a group of kids over when parents are not at home

RED LIGHT BEHAVIORS—STOP! DON'T!

- Drinking alcohol
- Smoking marijuana, doing any other drugs
- Scam parties
- Going to a deserted area
- Sex
- Violence such as hair pulling, grabbing, slapping
- Preventing a partner from moving freely
- Rape — forcing another to have sex

"Parties" are listed under two categories because there are different kinds of parties and it is up to you to Do a Reality Check to figure out what kind you are invited to.

A regular fun party might include dancing, eating, and games — maybe even kissing games. "Scam parties" are just the excuse that parents are given so the kids can get over to someone's house. From there, they might either drink, smoke, or have sex either in the house or off somewhere else. When it's time for pick-up, kids go back to the "party" site to meet their parents.

I'm sure you can see that a scam party can lead to all kinds of problems. It exists to cover up some other activity you know is wrong and unapproved. If you are invited to what you think or know is a scam party, Do a Reality Check and look at your options. You can always back out through Cool Communication.

If you get to a party and discover it is a scam party, use the secret weapons to make a good decision for yourself. You won't look like a wimp or a nerd if you choose to remove yourself from an unhealthy spot. Remember that you are the only one you have control over!

BE A GAME SHOW HOST!

People love to watch the television show, "The Dating Game." Three men or women sit in a protected area while someone of the opposite sex asks them questions. Based on the answers to these questions, the contestant selects one of the three for a date.

Sometimes the questions are silly, but most of the time the questions are designed to help the contestant learn as much as he/she can about the others. Questions range from "What is your ideal date?" and "Do you believe in kissing on the first date?" to "What date do you remember the most from your teenage years?"

One of the best ways for you to get a good idea of what a date really is, is to become like the game show host. You have a lot of information at your fingertips at home.

Interview your parents about *their* dates when they were teenagers. Some sample questions might be:

1. How old were you when you had your first date?
2. What did you do?

3. Did you single date or double date (go on a date with one other couple)?
4. Who planned the dates you went on, you or your date?
5. Were you ever nervous on a date? Why?
6. Did you ever ask a boy out? (For mom or other female)
7. What was the best date you ever had?
8. What was the worst date you ever had?
9. What kind of person attracted you?
10. Did you ever go out with someone and then find out that he/she was not like you thought at all? How did you find out? What did you do?

I'm sure you can think of more questions and if you listen carefully to the answers, more questions will pop up. If you can't interview a parent, then interview a grandparent, aunt, uncle, or older neighbor. You may find that not only do dates vary, but people will have some funny and interesting stories to share with you. This will help you form a more realistic picture of what a date can be.

Who Pays?

Once you have a clear idea of what a date is, you might wonder "Who pays for what?"

Strictly speaking, the person who does the inviting should pay for the date. If you, a boy, invite a girl to the movies, then you should be prepared to pay for the tickets, refreshments, and after-movie snacks, if there are going to be any.

There are many times today when girls ask boys to events that have a cost attached. The girl should then go prepared to handle the cost of the event and a snack. The boy should offer to help pay for refreshments — particularly if he is a big eater, as many adolescent boys are.

If the date consists of several boys and girls going out as a group together, rather than several couples, then they might agree to go "dutch" and have each person pay for themselves. If you want someone in the group to feel "special," you can then treat her to a candy or something else. One last tip — be sure to have enough money on you so you can call home in case of an emergency. You don't always know how a date will turn out and by keeping an extra fifty cents tucked away, you have the option of leaving if you need to.

If you use the secret weapons wisely, you can make dating one of the most enjoyable parts of your teenage years. Remember to Do a Reality Check: what exactly are the facts of the situation and how do you feel?

Look at all the options available and Take a Positive Risk: expanding your definition of a date and the number of people you have fun with keeps you in control. The more you learn about others through dating relationships, the more equipped you will be to eventually select the person who will be special enough to marry.

Finally, remember Cool Communication. Tell the other person what your feelings are. No one person's feelings and needs are more important than another's. You have to make decisions that you can live with for the rest of your life. You owe it to yourself to communicate that, whether another person agrees or disagrees.

CHAPTER 16

CAN I GET AIDS from FRENCH KISSINg?

"I know I'm young but I really love my boyfriend," said Brenda, fourteen. "When we're alone together and touching each other, my brain may say 'No' but my body says 'Yes, let's have sex.' My boyfriend, who's fifteen, says he's tired of me being a tease. I don't want to lose him but I'm afraid of AIDS. Can you get AIDS even with a condom? I don't want to get pregnant either. What about kissing? Can you get AIDS from French kissing?"

During your adolescent years, feelings and decisions about sexual matters take up a lot of your thoughts because your body changes have opened up a new phase of life. The only way to take control of your life and make good decisions regarding sex is by getting good information and looking at your options. Then make a decision that will be best for *you* over a long period of time.

In other words, Do a Reality Check and Take a Positive Risk.

At this time of your life when anything to do with sex is of particular interest and you're trying to learn all you can, it is easy to get the wrong information. And the wrong information can injure you for the rest of your life!

Most kids said that they get most of their sexual information from friends, television, or magazines. We have already talked about how the media distorts sex and relationships. Not only does the media distort the information on relationships, but it seems as though that's *all* they are concerned with. Every year there are an estimated 20,000 scenes suggesting sexual intercourse on prime time television. Magazines and radio would also lead you to believe that having sex is the way to be happy, popular, successful, glamorous, smart, and "cool."

Advertising uses sexual images because they send powerful

messages to the brain and body. The messages may be wrong but because people are interested in sex, they still pay attention and take the images in.

Not only is the image false, but it confirms your thoughts that you need to focus on sex all the time. Add that to the fact that a lot of your remaining information comes from your friends who are at your same stage of life and your misguided information is confirmed.

The truth of the matter is that adults spend 70% of their time on job-related activities and only 30% on social. When you consider that the 30% must then be divided into eating, sleeping, socializing, reading, bathing, doing chores, etc., you can see that sex really takes on a different perspective. It is a *part* of life, not the focus of it. And the way to success, popularity, beauty, health, and love comes from other sources.

But that doesn't answer your questions about sex, and today, with so many sexually transmitted diseases including AIDS, you need to do the biggest Reality Check of all concerning sex.

This is Reality!

Myth "Only homosexuals and drug users get AIDS. My girlfriend and I can't get it. We don't do drugs and we're only fourteen and fifteen."

Myth "You don't get pregnant if you're under fifteen years old."

Myth "Using condoms always prevents pregnancy and AIDS."

Those are just a few of the myths that kids pass on to each other. In order for you to Do a Reality Check, here are some facts.

- AIDS is a virus that anyone can get. It is spread mainly through sexual intercourse with an infected person, by using an infected needle or syringe, through impure blood products, or from a pregnant mother with AIDS to her unborn baby.

- Although the AIDS virus has been found to be present in tears or saliva, there are no recorded cases of it being spread this way. So while "dry" kissing is the safest, French or "wet" kissing (where the kissers touch tongues) has not been shown to spread AIDS.

- Every year, one out of six sexually active adolescents and teens catches a sexually transmitted disease. Teens who have been infected with AIDS have said that they weren't concerned about disease at the time; they just "went with the feelings of the moment."

- There are already more than 500 cases of AIDS reported among young people thirteen to eighteen years old. The cases among teens have risen 40% in the last two years and the rate continues to rise.

- Your partner may look and act completely normal, yet still carry the AIDS virus. Since the time it takes for the virus to make itself known in *your* system ranges between three and ten years, you can catch the virus at fourteen and not have it show up until you are twenty-four!

- In 1987, nearly 10,500 babies were born to girls ten to fourteen years old. It is estimated that this year over one million teens will get pregnant; nearly 33,000 of those will be fifteen years old and under.

- Fifty percent of those age 13-18, who say they have had sex, admitted that they have had three or more sexual partners. The more partners you have, the more likely it is that you will catch one of the many sexually transmitted diseases, including AIDS.

- Condoms are not always foolproof. They can leak and break. They are the second best protection against disease and pregnancy if you use them in combination with a spermicide (cream or jelly). The best defense against AIDS and pregnancy is to say "no" to having sex for now.

This is heavy stuff, but engaging in sex is a serious activity that can have a serious effect on you. Those who view sex as a recreational activity, like watching a video, are making a serious mistake in their reasoning. You can rewind a video you have made and edit out the mistakes. Once you have had sex with someone, you can never take it back.

"But," Brenda might say, "those facts are great. But I'm not a statistic—I'm a person with feelings and needs!"

WHAT ABOUT MY FEELINGS?

Let's go back and look at Brenda's situation. Doing a Reality Check, we see that Brenda is fourteen years old. What she is experiencing with her boyfriend is a strong sexual "chemistry."

You might normally think of chemistry as a subject in school, but people have what is called a "chemistry" too. While experts have tried to figure out just what causes it, what it boils down to is a strong pull of physical attraction between two people. You may feel a strong "chemistry" with one person and just a simple friendship with another.

Brenda and her boyfriend have a strong chemistry which is made stronger by doing things that excite their bodies even more. Brenda also says she loves her boyfriend and she's worried about losing him if she doesn't give in to his desire to have sex.

Brenda's head is telling her "no" for a good reason: she is not ready to have sex with anyone. Although the body may feel a strong pull, the *brain* controls what we do and when we do it. If she wants to stay in control of the situation, Brenda needs to continue to "feed" information to her brain, rather than ignore it or dull it with alcohol or drugs.

How will Brenda, or anyone, know when they are ready for sex? They are probably ready if they:

—Are not pressured into it.

—Are old enough to assume the responsibilities of a relationship and the consequences of their actions.

—Are not trying to improve a current relationship that's starting to cool.

—Have spent enough time with the person to get to know them and their sexual history. (You don't use sex to get to know a person — you get to know a person first, and then make the decision to have sex.)

—Can discuss the possibility of catching or passing on a sexually transmitted disease and understand the long-term effect on their life.

—Are not trying to prove that they are mature, macho, or sexy.

—Are sure that their reputation would not be hurt and that their partner will not humiliate them.

—Are comfortable with themselves as people and don't feel

guilty about getting involved in a sexual relationship.

—Are both mature enough to agree on a method of birth control and then practice it.

—Are both old enough and mature enough to agree on what both of them will do if the birth control method fails and the girl gets pregnant.

"But I don't want to be the last virgin in the school," says Brenda. "Everybody snickers if they think you're a virgin and they tell jokes. Besides, it will be so romantic!"

It might appear to be "romantic" to Brenda but for her boyfriend, it may be something else. Just as adolescent boys and girls are at different stages of physical development (Remember the party in Chapter Thirteen when the girls wanted romance and the boys wanted food?), they also have different attitudes towards sex and relationships.

What's Love Got to Do with It?

Here's what some adolescent girls say:

"He's so romantic. I love him and maybe we'll get married when we're old enough."

"I trust him. He said he'd never do anything to hurt me."

"He's so sexy and sweet. I don't want to be with anyone but him."

Here's what some adolescent boys say:

"Boy, I'm really horny."

"Hey man, of course I've had sex. Do you think I'm some sort of wimp?"

"Yeah, I love 'doing it' with her. If anything happens, I'll pay for the abortion."

One of the comments that was repeated in a number of the surveys filled out by girls was "Why do boys always seem to need more than one girlfriend?" Girls who become attracted to a guy tend to think in terms of a relationship. Why does he need more?

But at this stage of development a guy may be trying to figure out how to get his sexual questions answered and experience what he can. At this stage "having sex" is a long way from the love story ideal of "making love" that interests most girls. Kids may use these two terms to mean the same thing, but there are differences. Do you know what they are? Here are two diagrams:

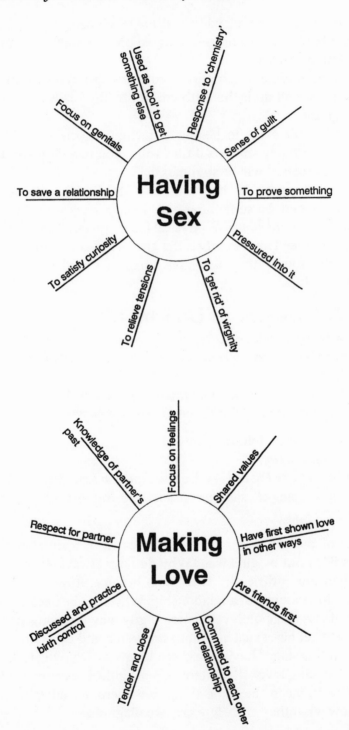

Having Sex

- Response to 'chemistry'
- Used as 'tool' to get something else
- Sense of guilt
- Focus on genitals
- To prove something
- To save a relationship
- Pressured into it
- To satisfy curiosity
- To 'get rid' of virginity
- To relieve tensions

Making Love

- Focus on feelings
- Knowledge of partner's past
- Shared values
- Respect for partner
- Have first shown love in other ways
- Are friends first
- Discussed and practice birth control
- Committed to each other and relationship
- Tender and close

During your adolescent years, you are learning who and what you are all about. Your sexuality is part of who you are. The first love you should feel is a love for yourself, your feelings, and your goals. Sometimes this is difficult since you make mistakes as you learn. Gradually, as your "house under construction" starts filling in, you can confidently move on and the mistakes become less important.

An unsuccessful, hurtful, or even harmful sexual relationship at this uncertain point in your life, however, can ruin more than your health and your school life. It can also wrongly influence how you feel about yourself.

When a school friend dumps you and starts hanging around with someone else, it hurts. You might cry or feel depressed and maybe even a little guilty — wondering why they grew away from you. But you can Do a Reality Check and realize that at your age, people change and grow in different directions. Your hurt feelings mend and you go on to other friendships.

When you are an adolescent, and you open yourself up to a sexual relationship and then that partner quite naturally moves on, the hurt can be crushing. Not only are the pain and guilt worse, but you have crossed a physical and emotional line that can never be erased. You have also risked your health and your reputation. All of those uncertain emotions and feelings about yourself are thrown down on the floor and stomped on. Another reality is that suicide is the second highest cause of death among teens and it is higher among sexually active teens than those who are not.

There is nothing wrong with being a "virgin." In fact, since we are living in times when people are rightly worried about AIDS and other sexually transmitted diseases, being a virgin is once again becoming something that is very special and respected in both boys and girls. Once again, you have the ability to take the power into your hands and make a choice. You can *choose* to wait until you are older to get involved in a sexual relationship. That is your right. Anyone who tries to make you think differently is wrong.

Going back to Brenda's decision, she Did a Reality Check. After getting good information on sex, AIDS, and pregnancy, she tried to focus on what she was feeling. She decided that if she said "yes" to her boyfriend, it was due to physical attraction and the desire to

keep him. She hadn't wanted to look bad in front of her friends —
like she couldn't "keep her man."

Brenda reviewed her options: Say yes, with all of the possible
consequences; or say "No, I'm not ready."

It would have been easy for Brenda to go along with her
boyfriend, but she Took a Positive Risk in favor of her gut feelings
and self-esteem. She reasoned that at her age, she would rather
risk losing a boyfriend than risk pregnancy, disease, or the guilt
that she would feel when the relationship was over. She felt that if
her boyfriend really loved her, he would respect her feelings even
if he didn't agree.

When she communicated her feelings and decisions to her
boyfriend, he got angry. Although Brenda told him that she really
loved him, he said she ought to prove it. Brenda rightly saw this as
more pressure for "sex" not "love" so she said no. Her boyfriend
left her and went on to someone else.

Brenda's story does have a happy ending, though. She did not
lose anything worthwhile in the relationship and she added to her
self-esteem because she Took a Positive Risk and made a decision
that was right for *her*. Brenda found a new boyfriend and they
have a good time dating and being affectionate with each other.
"We'll see what happens this time," she says with a grin.

Will I Ever Have Sex?

There are two more questions on middle schoolers' minds.

*"If I wait to have sex until I'm older, won't I still risk getting AIDS
from someone? At this rate, I'll never have sex!"*

And: *"What if I have already had sex? How can I stop?"*

Doing a Reality Check and learning the facts about AIDS and
other diseases are not meant to scare you away from ever having a
sexual relationship. Under the right circumstances and with the
right person, sex is a very beautiful part of a relationship. That
view of sex should come when both people are mature enough to
handle all of the strings that come along with it emotionally.

"Having sex" is easy. Dogs and cats and many other mammals
"do it" and don't give it much more thought. After reaching puberty, you are *physically* capable of having sex. What separates us

from those other mammals, as we discussed earlier, is that our *brain* gives us control over our feelings and our actions. Our ability to reason, to think things through to the final result and make a *choice* is an exciting power to exercise.

The physical act is easy. What is difficult is learning how to show affection, love, and caring in other ways. Hugging, kissing, talking, getting to know your partner by exploring their feelings, values, and attitudes are the parts of loving that you can be learning now. As you find yourself loving different people, and learning from them, you will also find that you are becoming more selective in who seems right for you. By your late teens, you will have passed through your adolescent years and be ready to make a more mature sexual choice.

If you have already had a sexual experience, you should not feel as though you have to continue. You have the right, at any time, to make a choice for yourself and say "no." Although you can't undo what has been done, you can put the decision back in your own hands.

We all need to feel loved and accepted. During adolescence, this is particularly true, especially on those days when nothing seems to go right. Take a Positive Risk and explore your options. If you want to share real love with someone, don't limit your definition to a physical act.

Chapter 17

You Can Be a Great Diver!

I am a scuba diver. I have dived in coral parks full of shark and barracuda. I have dived in fresh water caves where careless divers have lost their lives. And I have dived 145 feet below the surface of the water to see where the continental shelf drops straight down more than 2,500 feet.

Sometimes when people find out that I'm a diver, they act very surprised. They look at my five feet one inch height (when I stand up straight) and say, "How can a little thing like you be a diver?" They're surprised because they think of scuba diving in terms of being a sport that requires great *physical* strength. After all, there are air tanks, regulators, flippers, weight belts, wetsuits . . . lots of equipment.

But things aren't always what they seem.

Scuba diving actually requires more *mental* strength than physical. Sure, you *see* the equipment, the water, and Jacques Cousteau kicking hard through the water. But what you *don't see* makes the difference between a fun adventure and certain death.

When you dive, you go into unfamiliar territory. It is a new experience, with unfamiliar animals and dangers. Even if you have dived in that place before, waters and wildlife change, so there can always be unknown stresses and challenges. To be successful at meeting these challenges, you dive with your *brain*, not your *back*! In other words, you must always be prepared with a Plan B, in case something does not work out the way you expect it to. A good diver will carefully gather information about the diving site, plan the dive, and then dive the plan—and stick to it.

Adolescence is very much like scuba diving. Most of the "waters" (situations) that you enter *are* new and unfamiliar. Even the ones that are familiar can change as friends change and new challenges confront you.

People may look at adolescence and think of it mainly as the physical changes they can see — just like diving. But you know by now that adolescence also involves an even bigger mental and emotional challenge. Like a diver, to be successful, *you* need to be in control with a Plan B at all times. *Your* Plan B includes the three secret weapons: Do a Reality Check, Use Cool Communication, and Take a Positive Risk.

Whether you are dealing with family, friends, school, or members of the opposite sex, remember that *you have the power to make choices!* Look at all the facts and identify just what your feelings and needs are. Look at your options — there are always more than first appear. Then take a risk that will be positive and right for *you* even if it's not what everyone else is doing. And don't be afraid to communicate your feelings. Remember that nobody is a mindreader, although we sometimes expect them to be.

Growing through your adolescence takes practice, just as being a successful diver takes practice. At first, the equipment is so strange that there is a lot to think about. Even the way a diver breathes into the regulator is different in order to use the air properly. But with practice, pretty soon breathing, handling the equipment, and following safe diving procedure become part of the scuba diver. He or she doesn't have to think about it anymore. This leaves them free to concentrate on the beauty of the undersea world and meet the challenges they face.

It may feel strange to you to use the secret weapons at first. Sometimes they will work just right and you'll see results right away. Sometimes it will feel odd and your results will come a little slower. But with practice, they will become part of you and you won't have to think about them anymore.

Like a diver, this will leave you free to explore the world and relationships around you and enjoy your power to make choices in a new and exciting phase of life.

Index